Anthony Davis: The Incredible Story of One of Basketball's Most Dynamic Power Forwards

An Unauthorized Biography

By: Clayton Geoffreys

Table of Contents

Foreword

When the 2014-2015 NBA season kicked off, NBA analysts around the league were highly anticipating the meteoric rise of one particular big man: Anthony Davis. It's no surprise why when past MVP LeBron James has been quoted saying, "I think he's one of the elite players right now." At just twenty-one years old, Anthony Davis had quickly emerged as the face of the New Orleans Pelicans' franchise. A dominating big man with a unique skill set both offensively and defensively, Anthony Davis is not just the next superstar in the NBA, but a new definition for the role that big men will play in the NBA. Only a few select big men like Joakim Noah or Josh McRoberts can pass quite as well as Anthony Davis. It comes to no surprise though considering how Davis learned the game. Prior to an eight-inch growth spurt in high school, Davis was a point guard. Things have changed quite a bit since then and it will be incredibly exciting to continue to follow the highly anticipated career of one of the NBA's next great big men. Now a member of the Los Angeles Lakers, the Anthony Davis and LeBron James duo has already seen success with Davis winning his first championship ring in 2020. Thank you for purchasing *Anthony Davis: The Incredible Story of One of Basketball's Most Dynamic Power Forwards*. In this unauthorized biography, we will learn Anthony Davis' incredible life story and impact on the game of basketball. Hope you enjoy and if you do, please do not forget to leave a review!

Also, check out my website at claytongeoffreys.com to join my exclusive list where I let you know about my latest books. To thank you for your purchase, you can go to my site to download a free copy of *33 Life Lessons: Success Principles, Career Advice & Habits of Successful People*. In the book, you'll learn from some of the greatest thought leaders of different industries on what it takes to become successful and how to live a great life.

Cheers,

Clayton Geoffreys

Visit me at www.claytongeoffreys.com

Introduction

The power forward has always been one of the NBA's most unique positions because there was never a precise definition of what players in that role were supposed to do. Back in the days of Wilt Chamberlain and Bill Russell, power forwards were the smaller versions of centers. They rebounded and scored inside the paint, but not to the extent that centers were supposed to.

As time passed, power forwards became pseudo-centers in the sense that they were asked to do things that centers could do but were also tasked to do so much more. Some say that players such as Karl Malone and Charles Barkley redefined that role because they could play down low at the post and had the occasional perimeter game as well. Because they were more mobile and agile than most power forwards, it became a trend for power forwards to be more athletic and skilled than any other big men. Power forwards evolved even further when players such as Kevin Garnett, Tim Duncan, and Dirk Nowitzki took over the league.

For the majority of his career, Garnett was well-known because of his versatility. With his length and athleticism, he looked like a center with the skills of a small forward. Garnett could play from the perimeter with his sweet jump shot and was also an adept player in the paint. He went on to win a championship and numerous other individual awards as one of the best players to play at his position.

Regarded as probably the greatest power forward in league history, Tim Duncan played true to the tradition of that position. He was known more for his ability to score from the post than for his agility and athleticism. However, Duncan was more than a one-dimensional player. While he was best at posting up, he could take his man out from the paint with his patented banking jump shots and was always a terrific pick-and-roll player because of his mobility at that position. A two-time MVP himself, Duncan won five championships for the San Antonio Spurs and is regarded as one of the all-time great big men.

The power forward spot ultimately changed because of Dirk Nowitzki. Considered one of the best scorers and arguably the best international player in league history, Dirk became the prototype of today's floor-spacing big men. Nowitzki became known for his jump shot rather than his occasional inside scoring. He took his game well beyond the three-point line and was seemingly impossible to guard because of his length and skill as a shooter. Because teams feared his patented one-legged fadeaway shot so much, he used it to get the opening he needed from the post.

With those three players leading the way for the evolution of the power forward, the newer big men have transitioned their game away from the way guys of their position played three or so decades ago. Power forwards today have learned how to take their game away from the post, evolving to become adept at any situation, whether as scorers, defenders, or even playmakers. Among all of today's top power forwards, one of the most dangerous is Anthony Davis.

Dissecting Anthony Davis' life journey will give a better appreciation for his rise to stardom and how he is considered one of the all-time best at his position. It is only after a careful examination of his life that you can fully understand what he has become today. It was how he developed from his childhood days to his dominance in the NBA that dictated how he became such a versatile and great player at the power forward spot.

Anthony Davis is one of the most intriguing players to have ever played in the NBA. Just by looking at his appearance, you would never be able to tell that he was not always that enormous while growing up. Back when Davis was still in high school, he stood at 6'3" until he had an eight-inch growth spurt. Unlike most players who had large growth spurts, the once-little point guard retained his dribbling and playmaking skills. I guess you could say that Davis *literally* took his talent to new heights.

Anthony Davis attended a high school that was not well-known for producing the best basketball prospects. During his prep years, he did not receive much attention until his rapid growth spurt. Davis was used to shooting jump shots when driving in the lane, but he would then start dunking on people. A few years before that, he could barely even reach the rim.

However, he never really focused on blocking shots or backing down his opponent on the offensive end. He knew he had his work cut out for him and was ready for the challenge. Davis understood that he had to learn how to become an inside presence, and quickly tried to do so. While swatting shot after shot, and often stealing the ball from the opposing guards, Davis started to pick up speed.

Davis joined the Kentucky Wildcats for college. He made an excellent choice and joined a team surrounded by great supporting members. He was not used to that kind of experience because he had never played on great teams while competing. Nevertheless, the Kentucky team was perfect for him because they shared the ball and played true team defense.

Coach John Calipari played a crucial role in Davis' evolution. The tough and gritty coach expected a lot from his team, players, and more importantly, his big man. Davis went on to lead the team to an NCAA title, earning Most Outstanding Player and setting new records along the way. NBA scouts were now taking notice of the massive power forward with the infamous unibrow.

His unibrow was so iconic while playing that fans often held up signs and chanted "Fear the Brow," among other things. It became his trademark look and nickname. It was what set him apart from a physical standpoint from the rest of the big men and added instant recognition that only helped to boost his growing popularity even further. However, it was his game and potential as a future star that made him an appealing prospect to the NBA.

In 2012, Davis was drafted as the first overall pick by the New Orleans Hornets (now Pelicans). He was set to join a New Orleans team that was still recovering from the Chris Paul era. But with Anthony Davis coming in, the Hornets were expected to improve on their chances to rebuild the franchise and once again become contenders in the NBA.

Because Anthony Davis was already so promising at that point, he was even selected to take part in the 2012 Olympics as a member of Team USA, where he would play alongside all-time greats such as Kobe Bryant, LeBron James, and Kevin Durant. The team won the gold medal in dominant fashion that year, and with Anthony Davis (who had not even played a single NBA game) playing a limited role. Exposed to the sheer beauty and excellence of teaming up with the greatest players on the planet, Anthony Davis was certainly set to forge a promising NBA career for himself.

At first, Davis was coveted for his defense and athletic versatility at the power forward spot. His offense was still a work in progress, however. The skills and the talent were already there, but it was evident that he still needed to grow. He had a good rookie year but was still far from fulfilling his potential.

But from his second year and onwards, Davis started to grow into his potential remarkably well. Not only did he dominate on the defensive end but he also showed an offensive versatility heretofore unseen from a man of his size. Davis dribbled the ball and shot jumpers like he was a guard. He could move and get off the floor so fluidly that he looked like he was 6'6" instead of 6'10". And best of all, he still played how a power forward should play.

Using his athleticism and physical attributes, Anthony Davis became the culmination of how several generations of power forwards before him had developed and advanced the position. He had the fluidity and mobility of Karl Malone, the length and athletic versatility of Kevin Garnett, the perimeter shooting of Dirk Nowitzki, and the inside skills of Tim Duncan. It was as if generations of the league's best power forwards were all mashed up to form the player who eventually became Anthony Davis.

However, despite all of Davis's skills and superstar prowess, he took time to become the most successful player. He proved himself capable of leading a team to the playoffs, but always ended up getting disappointing losses while he was with the New Orleans Pelicans. Indeed, AD was a lone star in New Orleans, and he struggled against the best teams in the Western Conference because the Pelicans were not as well-built as the other squads. But perhaps the biggest problem that Davis struggled with was his injury history, as there were a lot of moments wherein he ended up getting injured during crucial points of the season.

After several years of being a lone star in New Orleans, Davis finally got to team up with DeMarcus Cousins via a trade that brought the massive center to the Pelicans. Known as the best center in the NBA, Cousins gave Davis the star partner he desperately needed to get over the hump. Since the two big men had found little to no success as winners in their respective separate careers, it was time for them to join forces and dominate the league. And that was exactly what they did.

This tandem of the world's best power forward and the league's best center became, for all intents and purposes, the best frontcourt the league had seen since Tim Duncan and David Robinson.

However, the partnership was short-lived. Sadly, Cousins suffered a season-ending injury just a year later. As such, Davis was once again the lone star in New Orleans and moved up to the center position due to the absence of his star teammate. When Cousins ultimately left the team, Anthony Davis became a solo artist once again, which ultimately forced him to think about his status in New Orleans.

During the offseason of 2019, Anthony Davis was traded to the Los Angeles Lakers to become the team's latest star big man. Teaming up with LeBron James, Davis now had the opportunity to play with someone more accomplished than he was at that time. Best of all, he had a chance to continue the big-man legacy that the Lakers of yesteryears were able to carry with so much pride and dignity.

In just his first season with the Lakers, Davis proved himself to be a difference-maker because he transformed the entire squad and turned it into one of the best teams in the league. Teaming up with LeBron allowed Davis to run free on the court because he now had one of the greatest players of all

Chapter 1: Childhood and Early Life

Anthony Marshon Davis, Jr. was born to Anthony Davis, Sr. and Erainer Davis on March 11, 1993, in Rochelle, Illinois. He has two siblings named Lesha and Antoinette, who are twins. They grew up in the rough neighborhood of Englewood, Chicago, which is famous for being a dangerous place.

Erainer and Anthony Sr. did their best to provide for the family and keep them safe. Not only did they give their children shelter and food but they also always emphasized the importance of education. For them, education was vital to make something out of yourself. They continually reminded Anthony and his sisters to value their education since it would help them become better people. The young Anthony took their advice to heart and excelled in his studies.

Along with his studies, Anthony was very interested in sports. He loved baseball, and having grown up in Chicago, he was naturally a White Sox fan. In football, however, he was surprisingly a fan of the Green Bay Packers rather than the Chicago Bears. Meanwhile, his father was a die-hard Bears fan, and so they often made wagers between each other whenever both NFL teams squared off. Davis claimed that he always won the bet because the Bears did not have a great team. Davis's favorite basketball player of all time is Michael Jordan, and if he had to pick a 4-man 3-on-3 team, it would include His Airness, Magic Johnson, Wilt Chamberlain, and himself.

Anthony loved playing basketball growing up. However, his parents knew that sometimes, the courts of Englewood were just too violent. Thus, his parents installed a basketball ring in their backyard. Davis was a humble and laid-back child in his youth. Always a fun-loving and humorous individual,

Davis loves his family and enjoys spending quality time with them. His family is a crucial part of his life, and he is determined to create a better life for them by virtue of his own success.

As a boy, Davis did not honestly envision himself ever making it to the NBA, but he also knew that he needed to become successful so that he could take his family out of the ghetto and move into a nicer area. This ambition helped Davis to get motivated with his academics and athletics. Although he was not a giant growing up, he still managed to compete. He was a natural point guard who loved to shoot the ball in the 3-point corner. However, it was not until high school that Davis had a growth spurt of eight inches that changed his future.

Chapter 2: High School Years

Anthony Davis attended Perspectives High School, his school since 6th grade. The school was not well-known for its athletics and belonged to a division of the Chicago Public High School League known as the Blue Division. There was not much press or media coverage of their athletics since they competed at a very low level. This did not matter much to Davis, however, since he was primarily focused on his education.

Perspectives High School had two teachers in each class to provide more guidance to the students. The school is so successful that it has a 95% success rate for graduating students. This speaks volumes about this school, especially considering that it is located in an area where violence and peer pressure are still prevalent.

Anthony played on the basketball team for his four years in high school. His school did not have much of a team, and it always had a losing record. To add insult to injury, it did not even have a gym or a hoop outside that was reliable. This forced them to take a bus to a church or recreational center where practices were never guaranteed. The school simply did not have the budget for the team, which is why they were not able to practice all the time. In fact, the primary reason for their losing records was the issue that they could not even practice regularly.

Sophomore Year

As a sophomore, Davis stood at 6'2" and was playing as the team's point guard. Opposing teams took notice and called Davis the skinny point guard who liked to shoot threes from the corner. Miraculously, Davis would shoot up an astounding 8" over a short period of time, eventually reaching an adult height of 6'10" when he was 17 years of age. But during his sophomore year, he added an incredible 5" to his frame.

People were afraid that Anthony was going to have aches and pains trying to figure out how to play with so much more height, especially considering how rapidly the change had occurred. Fortunately, he did not have any knee pains from his massive growth spurt and amazingly retained most of his point guard abilities. However, he was no longer bringing up the ball and was more of a post threat or ran the court in transition.

His new length and height made it easier to score, steal the ball, block shots, and rebound, all of which came naturally for him. He had a knack for timing and began to rack up the blocked shots at a breakneck pace. Before his growth spurt, only one Division 1 team had offered him a scholarship. Cleveland State offered him a spot on their roster as a shooting guard—but that quickly changed as he started to get more attention.

Junior Year

As a junior, Anthony was still growing, albeit more slowly. He began the season at 6' 7" and ended at 6' 8". He felt blessed to have been graced with an abundance of height without the usual accompanying knee pains. His dad was not worried that Anthony was not getting enough exposure to generate more college offers, but in the middle of his junior year, his family considered transferring him to a nearby basketball powerhouse. However, his head coach later advised that if Anthony were good enough, scouts would find *him*. This advice proved to be correct, as Davis finally started to receive offers once the whispers about him began circulating.

Senior Year

Davis' team finished with a lousy record for three consecutive years, and his talent went virtually unnoticed until his senior year. After connecting with the AAU Team, MeanStreets, a team that often traveled to play other opposing teams, more scouts were in attendance. Davis did not get much coverage until April 2010 when Syracuse University offered him a full scholarship. ESPN as well as many prominent basketball names were now taking notice of Anthony Davis, and he was regarded as one of the top prospects in the nation. Although his ranking differed from source to source, he could finally play against better competition. Coincidentally, one of his primary rivals for the top spot was his teammate, Austin Rivers.

Davis got invited to numerous camps and tournaments facing the best players across the nation. He knew that it was imperative to stand out if he wanted to get the respect that he deserved. That summer, he played at the Nike Global Challenge, where he scored 23 points and grabbed 9 rebounds in the opening game.

After much contemplation, Davis decided to take his talents to the University of Kentucky, where he would play under legendary coach John Calipari. Interestingly, rumors started to swirl about this time that Anthony's dad had requested the Wildcats pay them $200,000 for his son to play for them. As some people might recall, this caused quite a stir and was heavily frowned upon. However, the Davis family refuted this claim, even though the *Sun-Times* refused to back down from spreading these rumors. This eventually tainted the *Sun-Times* name when their allegations proved to be unfounded and all the commotion started to die down. Certainly, there were compelling reasons why Kentucky was a terrific choice for Davis. Ultimately, his decision to commit to the Wildcats gave him the opportunity to take his talents to a whole new level.

In high school, meanwhile, Anthony Davis received numerous basketball awards including being named to the 2011 McDonald's All-American Game and the Jordan Brand Classic.

In the McDonald's game, where he played in front of his hometown at the United Center, Davis posted 14 points, 6 rebounds, 2 steals, and 4 blocks. He was named co-MVP along with Bob McAdoo in the Jordan Brand Classic after posting 29 points, 11 rebounds, and 4 blocks.

All things considered, Anthony Davis had a fantastic high school career despite the slow start. His additional height allowed him to become a dominant force and elevated him to a top NBA prospect. What is perhaps most surprising about it was that he accomplished all of this while attending a Blue Division school that did not even have a place to practice. This demonstrates Davis's character and staunch determination. He was well on his way to further educating himself and helping his family move out of Englewood.

Chapter 3: College Career

Anthony Davis chose the University of Kentucky not only because of their basketball program but also because the university offered the academic courses that he most wanted to pursue. Of course, the university has an excellent reputation in basketball, but they also offered a PT or high-school coaching program, so Davis made the right choice.

Many might perceive head coach John Calipari as a bit of a nut, but the flamboyant Hall-of-Famer has a track record that shows his system works. Anthony had a great relationship with his coach from day one and took all his advice to heart. In an interview, he described Coach Calipari as a very passionate man, which might be a gentle way to describe his larger-than-life character.

The fact was, Calipari often yelled and grabbed players if they were not listening. Nevertheless, many players who came from his system ended up becoming not just good but *great* NBA players. Indeed, Calipari had a well-known knack for discovering and honing basketball talent. Moreover, many of his players entered the NBA draft.

Calipari's squads have featured many players who found careers in the NBA, with several players going in the first round. This impressive list includes Marcus Camby from UMass (second selection in the 1996 NBA Draft), Derrick Rose (first selection in the 2008 NBA Draft), and John Wall (first selection in the 2010 NBA Draft). As of this writing, about 40 players coached by Calipari in NCAA Division I basketball from UMass, Memphis, and Kentucky have found their way into the NBA. His teams had 16 total appearances in the NCAA National Championship Tournament.

Thus, when Davis joined the Kentucky Wildcats in 2011, he found himself surrounded by talented players, which was something he was not used to on his high school team. And when the Wildcats started to string together a few wins in a row, Davis found himself in awe. It was a transcendental time for Davis to finally be in a competitive environment and not feel like the big fish in a small pond like he was used to in Chicago, Illinois.

During his freshman year, Davis posted monster numbers, especially on the defensive end. In his first game in a Wildcats uniform on November 11, 2011, he scored 23 points, grabbed 10 rebounds, dished out 3 assists, and blocked 5 shots in Kentucky's win over Marist. Davis did that while shooting 10 out of 13 from the field and 3 for 3 from the line. But what made that incredible stat line even more impressive was that he managed to get these figures in less than 24 minutes of playing time. The Wildcats had one of the deepest teams at the college level, and Davis led the pack. Marquis Teague had 16 points, Doron Lamb and Michael Kidd-Gilchrist had 15 points each, and Kyle Wiltjer had 14 points.

In their next game on November 15th, they were against much fiercer competition—the Kansas Jayhawks. That game was their first real test of the early season. Unlike the previous match wherein they dominated, Kansas was giving them a run for their money. However, Davis and his teammates proved to be too much as they defeated the Jayhawks, too.

Davis did not have as many shot attempts against the Jayhawks, scoring 14 points after eight attempts and making six field goals. But Davis also grabbed six rebounds, two steals, and swatted an impressive seven shots. It was clearly his defensive prowess that helped his team win games. In spite of Kansas having a great roster that included Tyshawn Taylor and Thomas

Robinson, it was Anthony Davis who anchored the defense, which was a telling precursor to what fans would later see in the postseason.

While Davis had many fantastic individual performances during the season, he did not transition into college as smoothly as people might have thought. Although his stats were impressive, Davis admitted that he struggled to play on the low block at the offensive end. He was not used to backing down players who were around his size. At this early point in his career, Davis still had not developed footwork or isolation moves. He confessed that much of his progress had stalled because he was not yet sure of himself on the offensive end.

In Kentucky's third game of the season on November 19th, Davis only had two field-goal attempts for two points and made one free throw out of four to have three points in 23 minutes during a win over Penn State.

Davis did a little bit better on November 20th, when he had 11 points after shooting 4 out of 6 from the field and 3 out of 5 from the foul line in the Wildcats' win over Old Dominion. He also had nine rebounds, three blocks, and one assist. After that performance, Davis had 12 points with a perfect 4 out of 4 from both the field and the free-throw line in 25 minutes during Kentucky's 88-40 win over Radford on November 23rd. In this game, Davis collected six rebounds, four blocks, and one steal.

Despite his early-season struggles, after a few games with Calipari wanting to go to Davis on the low block, he started to develop more confidence. In fact, he gained so much confidence that he began to ask his coach for lower block plays. And, once he had gained confidence, there was not much that an opponent could do to stop him. Davis became a freak athlete standing at 6'

10" with a 7' 3" wingspan that made him suitable for defending opposing shots and collecting rebounds.

As mentioned before, the Wildcats had quite an impressive roster. It was so remarkable that a few of his Wildcat teammates even joined Davis in the NBA. Those players are Michael Kidd-Gilchrist, who was considered a higher prospect going into college, Terrence Jones, who now plays for the Houston Rockets and had a breakout season last year, and Marquis Teague, who is the brother of Jeff Teague and played for the Chicago Bulls. Terrence Jones and MKG are known to be stout defenders, and they made it extremely difficult for the competition to score.

To start the season, they went on a 10-game winning streak, and there were some strong games for Davis, including 13 points and 12 rebounds in the team's 87-63 win over Portland on November 26th, where he also had 4 blocks and 2 steals. In the very next game on December 1st, Davis had another 15 points and 15 rebounds along with an impressive 8 blocks during the team's win over St. John's.

On December 3rd, the Wildcats faced another tough test with perennial tournament team North Carolina, who was ranked fifth in the nation at that time and had a roster that featured Tyler Zeller and Harrison Barnes. It was not Davis's best game, since he only had seven points, but he had nine rebounds to go along with two blocks and two steals. Kidd-Gilchrist led Kentucky with 17 points and 11 rebounds to give them the win over the Tar Heels. This winning streak had some great team performances, and individual stars showed that this Kentucky squad was capable. However, they were about to face their first road test on December 10th against the always-formidable Indiana Hoosiers.

The Wildcats ultimately lost to Indiana in a nail-biter. Davis struggled to get scoring attempts, finishing the game with only six points after making three out of four field goals. He did have a good amount of rebounds, however—seven of them on defense as well as three steals and three blocks. The game was kept close by Lamb's 19 points, while Kidd-Gilchrist had 16 points and 9 rebounds.

After this disappointing loss, Kentucky immediately bounced back and commenced an even more impressive streak, winning more than 20 games in dominating fashion to reclaim their top ranking amongst both the Coaches and Associated Press polls.

The first step to that was taken on December 17th, when Kentucky defeated Chattanooga at home. Anthony Davis had one of his best games overall with 14 points after making 7 out of 11 from the field. He also had a season-best 18 rebounds, 13 of which came while playing defense, to compliment 5 blocks and a steal. A few games later against Loyola Maryland on December 22nd, Davis had 15 points and 11 rebounds in Kentucky's win. Then, on December 28th, Davis had another double-double with 10 points, 13 rebounds, and 6 blocks in a win over Lamar.

Just before the end of 2011 and entering the 2012 half of the season, Davis scored 18 points while collecting 10 rebounds in a win over the Louisville Cardinals within 27 minutes of action on the court. He had 6 blocks and 3 steals while making most of his points from the foul line, netting 12 out of 13 free throws in addition to 3 out of 4 from the field. Eighteen points were his season high for scoring at the time, but Davis topped that with his first game by surpassing the 20-point mark. He made 9 out of 11 field goals on January 3rd in a win over Arkansas-Little Rock, finishing with 22 points and 16 rebounds. He also blocked three shots during the game.

The Wildcats continued their strong performances into the Southeastern Conference (SEC) schedule, and Anthony Davis continued to shine, essentially collecting double-doubles like baseball cards. In his first SEC game, Davis scored 12 points and collected 10 rebounds while blocking 7 shots on defense during the team's win at home against the South Carolina Gamecocks on January 7th. A few days later on January 11th, Davis scored another 14 points on the road against the Auburn Tigers. It was only their second road game of the season at this point.

That was followed up with another strong performance from Davis on the road against the Tennessee Volunteers on January 14th. He shot 7 out of 10 from the field and 4 of 5 from the free-throw line to have 18 points to go along with 8 rebounds, 4 blocked shots, and 2 steals in 35 minutes in Knoxville, Tennessee.

On January 17th, Davis scored 27 points after making 10 out of 12 field goals along with 7 out of 8 free throws for a total of 27 points in the team's victory over the Arkansas Razorbacks. He also had 14 rebounds and 7 blocked shots on defense. He did all of this within 36 minutes of what turned out to be his best game of the season for a team that was only growing stronger. A few months later, Davis made 10 out of 11 field goals and 8 out of 9 from the foul stripe to score a season-high 28 points in 37 minutes during the Wildcats' victory over the Vanderbilt Commodores.

However, it was this same Vanderbilt team that they had defeated twice in February that gave them their second loss of the season on March 11th. It was a game where Davis struggled from the field, converting only 4 out of 9 field goals and 4 out of 8 from the foul line for 12 points and 10 rebounds. The loss to the Commodores put an end to the Wildcats' 24-game winning streak. However, it proved to be the team's last loss of the season, as they put together one final winning streak when it mattered most.

Their two very lengthy winning streaks alone made the Kentucky Wildcats qualify for the NCAA National Championship Tournament. They were ranked No. 1 in the South Regional and squared off against Western Kentucky, which won the Sun Belt conference tournament for the automatic berth into the tournament, despite having a record of 16-18.

On March 15th, Davis convincingly put up 16 points, grabbed 9 rebounds, and swatted 7 shots, leading the Wildcats to the next round where they faced Iowa State, a team that had decent success with 23 wins and a 12-6 record in the Big 12 Conference. Fortunately, the Wildcats defeated their opponent in a lopsided victory on March 17th. Davis had 15 points with 12 rebounds, 5 assists, and blocked 2 shots.

Their next matchup proved to be a great challenge for them. Indiana was one of the only two teams that had given the Wildcats a loss on their record, and they had an impressive 27-9 record coming out of a strong Big Ten Conference. With that loss in the back of their minds, they knew that fourth-seeded Indiana was not to be taken lightly.

This game was an intense battle with both juggernauts exchanging blows, but the Wildcats came out on top with a win over Indiana on March 23rd in the Sweet 16 round of the National Championship Tournament. It was not the best performance for Davis, since he only had nine points after making just two field goals and five out of six free throws. However, he grabbed 12 rebounds and blocked 3 shots.

It was evident that this Wildcats team was not the same team that fell to Indiana earlier in the season. They had evolved not just individually but also as a team. They advanced to the next round, which was the National Quarterfinals, to go up against Baylor University, which had an impressive 30-8 record—one of three teams out of the Big 12 Conference to have 30 or more wins.

On March 25th, Davis had an excellent performance against Baylor. He shot well from the field, making six out of nine, and made six out of eight at the free-throw line as well. However, he did get into some foul trouble. If it had not been for the foul trouble, the score might not have been so close. Nevertheless, the Wildcats got their act together and defeated Baylor with Davis scoring 18 points, grabbing 11 rebounds, getting 2 steals, and blocking 6 shots. The Kentucky defense proved to be too much for Baylor's offensive play to overcome, reinforcing the adage, "defense wins championships."

Kentucky advanced to the National Semifinals—better known to sports fans as the Final Four—against Louisville. Louisville was a well-rounded team coached by the infamous Rick Pitino. Their squad, consisting of Kyle Kuric, Russ Smith, Chris Smith, Chane Behanan, Gorgui Dieng, and Peyton Siva, allowed the Cardinals to get far into the tournament. They already had 30 wins for that season, which meant that they were a little more robust than the team Kentucky had faced at the end of 2011. They defeated Michigan State to get to the semifinals.

However, unfortunately for Louisville, Kentucky was too much for them to handle. Davis and his Wildcats prevailed once again and advanced to the National Finals. Davis almost posted identical numbers from his previous game against Louisville. He made 18 points after making 7 out of 8 field goals and 4 of 6 from the foul line. He also collected 14 rebounds and blocked 5 shots. With Davis taking charge as one of the defensive stars for the Wildcats, his eyes were focused on the championship.

Their final obstacle was Kansas, whom they had managed to defeat by 10 points earlier in the season. However, this Jayhawks team led the Big 12 with a 16-2 conference record and had compiled a 32-6 record leading up to the National Championship game. However, despite Kansas coming into the Finals with an impressive record of their own and having defeated Ohio State in their own Final Four matchup, there was much confidence among the Wildcats knowing that they had earned a crucial victory over the Jayhawks earlier in the season. It was make-or-break for the Kentucky Wildcats, and it was the championship that their head coach had been seeking since arriving at the Kentucky campus.

On April 2nd, Davis was not spectacular on the offensive. He only made one shot out of 10 from the field and finished with 6 points. However, it was never his offensive game that made him one of Kentucky's best players on the team. Davis was doing what he did best and made up for his lack of points with 16 rebounds, 5 assists, 3 steals, and 6 blocks. It was a close game, but the basketball gods favored the Wildcats.

The Kentucky Wildcats now had the honor to bring home another trophy to add to their collection. This was one of Anthony's most memorable moments, and his family could not have been prouder. All of his hard work and dedication had paid off. He was named Most Outstanding Player in the NCAA Tournament and also racked up an impressive line of awards.

He was named first team All-American while also being named the Men's College Basketball Player of the Year by *Sporting News* magazine. He was also awarded by several different organizations, including being the first Kentucky player in more than 40 years to earn the Naismith College Player of the Year Award just a few days after receiving the John R. Wooden Award. That award is given annually to outstanding players in both men's and women's college basketball. Other honors he received included being a first team All-American player while also being named the Freshman of the Year by the U.S. Basketball Writers of America, which also gave him the Oscar Robertson Trophy as their Player of the Year.

When you look at Davis's finals numbers for the season, you will understand why he was showered with all these awards. He made 62.3% of his shots from the field and averaged 14.2 points per game. He also averaged 10.4 rebounds, 4.7 blocks, 1.4 steals, and 1.3 assists. Davis led the NCAA in blocked shots with 186 for the entire 2011-2012 season and set records for blocked shots as a freshman. Davis could have had no prouder moment. He earned the right to raise that trophy and set his sights on a bigger stage that many of the players whom Coach Calipari had mentored were able to reach—the NBA.

While Anthony Davis was a clear one-and-done player whose primary goal was to go to college to become a winner and increase his stock as an NBA prospect, he already did a lot in his lone year with the Wildcats. He was only a freshman but he was already the best defensive presence in the entire collegiate ranks, as there was no one that could get a good shot inside the paint whenever he was patrolling nearby. Davis showcased defensive abilities and versatile skills at a very young age. And that was why he was able to translate his performances throughout his freshman year into a championship.

Not a lot of players could say that they were already the best player on the best team in college in just their freshman year, but Davis had the right to say just that after winning a championship as the most dominant two-way force on Kentucky during that championship run. But the best part about it was that he was also the best player in the entire collegiate ranks, and not many one-and-done prospects can claim to be better than all the other college players in the entire country. So, as Anthony Davis was about to leave the program after his lone year as a Wildcat, there was no doubt that he was set to enjoy a fruitful NBA career as one of the hottest young prospects the league had seen in a long while.

Chapter 4: NBA Career

Getting Drafted

The 2012 NBA Draft had plenty of talent when it came to the 10 best prospects of that class. Kentucky freshman forward Michael Kidd-Gilchrist showed promise as a defender because of his size, athleticism, and versatility. Florida's Bradley Beal was also a favorite to land in the top five because of his shooting and scoring prowess at the guard position.

Out of the crop of the best prospects, two others also eventually turned out to be All-Stars. Point guard Damian Lillard developed into one of the best scoring playmakers in the entire NBA. Meanwhile, Andre Drummond's combination of size and athleticism made him a terrific center even in the professional league. However, out of all of those talented players, the youngster Anthony Davis stood head and shoulders above the rest concerning talent and potential.

From a physical standpoint alone, Anthony Davis was already a fearsome future NBA star. At 6'10", he had the right size for an NBA big man who could shuffle between the power forward and center positions. However, it was his length that made him coveted based on his measurements. The 19-year-old was coming into the NBA with a wingspan that measured nearly 7'5".[i] He rivaled Kevin Garnett in terms of his body structure.

Even though Anthony Davis was coming in as an impressive physical specimen because of his height and length, what made him an even better prospect was the fact that he did not seem like a man who stood 6'10" and with a large wingspan. He runs the floor well for his size. At times, he even looked like a guard because of his fluidity, mobility, and speed on the floor. Impressively, he was also measured to have a vertical leap of nearly 36".

Because of his fluidity, overall explosiveness, and smooth mobility on the floor, Davis's athleticism and measurements made him arguably the most physically gifted athletic prospect of the past decade. What was even better was that Anthony Davis was never shy about using his physical tools and athleticism to his advantage, whether it was on the defensive end or as a scorer.

Davis always used his terrific length and explosive leaping ability to great effect on the offensive end. Arguably the most efficient scorer in the nation in only his freshman year, he was converting nearly 70% of his two-point attempts because of the quality of the shots he was taking. Davis uses all his physical tools to his advantage to finish well over the top of the defense. In college, he was an easy target for the lob because there was always a chance for him to finish the basket on the catch. When finishing non-post attempts, Anthony Davis converted 80% of his shots. When guards gave him drop passes and lobs, it was a likely conclusion that it would end in a basket for Davis.

Ranking on top of the NCAA in dunks, Anthony Davis was always an easy target because of how quickly he could jump off his feet. Unlike other big men and high leapers, Davis did not always need to gather himself. Even without momentum, he could jump higher than anybody from a standstill position. That was why he was extremely efficient as a finisher and scorer off offensive rebounds.

However, Davis was not always content with drop passes or lobs. He sometimes tried to take matters into his own hands. Knowing that he had the quickness and athletic advantage over most big men, Davis knew when and how to face his opponents up from the post to try to take his defender off the dribble. Using the footwork he developed when he was still a guard in high school, he could even get his defenders off-balanced down in the low post.[i]

Whenever John Calipari and the Kentucky Wildcats needed a sure basket, the simplest way was to find Anthony Davis near the rim. He could jump over any of his defenders. And if that wasn't possible, he had the length to finish over any outstretched arms. Davis was coming into the draft as one of the most impressive finishers in recent years.

On the rebounding end, Davis also uses his physical gifts to his advantage. With his quick-leaping ability and his mobility, he can get into the best positions for rebounds. Because he is so long and athletic, Davis can even get rebounds he is not in a position to grab. In the NCAA, he was more active as an offensive rebounder due to his great timing and positioning. Because of his excellent offensive rebounding ability, he ranked as one of the best at scoring off of putbacks. His soft hands and natural ability to guide the ball back in also helped in that regard.

For all of his abilities as an efficient and athletic scorer, it was on the defensive end where Anthony Davis truly made a difference in the college basketball setup.[i] He knew how to use his length and explosive leaping ability to make the game trend in his team's favor. No other defensive player affected the game as much as Davis did for the Kentucky Wildcats.

Davis led the entire nation in blocks per game after averaging nearly five swats. He was never the tallest or the longest rim protector, but he did make a difference because he knew how to use the physical tools he was given. Using his length and quick hops, he could get to opponents' shots with relative ease. There was only so much that long arms and a high jumping ability could do. Davis was always able to block shots because of his terrific timing and intensity. He owned the defensive end of the floor because he poured in all of his focus to protect the basket.

Even when Davis was not blocking shots, he knew how to make life tougher for opposing offenses by being an intimidating figure inside the paint. His quickness and mobility helped him cover more ground to protect the basket even when he was not in the best position to try to contest shots. Because of his timing and awareness, he was one of the best at helping from the weak side to block or contest attempts that already seemed open. Despite his aggressive nature at protecting the basket, Anthony Davis blocked shots and contested attempts without fouling.

Rim protection was not Anthony Davis's best asset as a defender. While playing the power forward and the center position for Kentucky, he was also terrific at covering the pick-and-roll because he was just as mobile and agile as a guard. Despite being able to move as well as guards do, his length made it more difficult for perimeter players to get to the basket or even put up long jumpers because Davis could easily contest them with his long arms.[i]

Davis was also known for not quitting on a defensive play. Not always as quick as some of the nation's fastest perimeter players, he sometimes found himself getting beaten off the dribble. Despite that, Davis used his quickness and wingspan to block or contest shots off the recovery. He could affect shots even from behind the offensive player because of his sheer will and aggressiveness as a defender.

Though Davis's sheer length and athletic abilities made him the top prospect of that year's NBA draft, he still had some weaknesses to work on before he could make the transition from college's best player to a superstar in the big league. For a player as talented as he was, there were only a few weaknesses that stood out for Davis.

One of his glaring weaknesses was his skinny frame. During his youth as merely a guard, he was always thin. When he started to grow, he could not fit into his 6'10" frame and remained skinny when he joined the Kentucky Wildcats. Because he lacked the heft to be able to compete with bigger players, he was often exposed by stronger power forwards and centers.

On the offensive end, Davis struggled as a post-up player. He only averaged only about one post-up play a game because he lacked the strength and skill to take his man down on the low block. During the rare times that Davis did try to score from the post, he only scored or got fouled on 25% of those attempts when he tried to take his man down low.[i] Because he was not a post-up threat, he did not have many scoring opportunities and was only able to score off lobs, drop passes, or offensive rebounds. Again, the reason why he was not always able to score down at the post was because of his lack of strength. He could not get the best inside position or push defenders down low.

As a defender, Anthony Davis sometimes struggled in one-on-one situations down at the low block. Because of his thin frame and lack of upper and lower body strength, there was only so much he could do against bigger and stronger power forwards and centers that pushed him around inside the paint. Against the much bigger and more mature NBA bodies, Davis might find himself getting pushed around more often than he did back in college.

While Anthony was still basically raw and unpolished at 19 years old coming into the NBA, it was more about the *potential* he had. He may have been a skinny player, but his shoulder width and frame made it look like he could still grow bigger and stronger. Kevin Garnett, a player whom he was often compared to, was a skinny kid during his first few years in the NBA as well, but he eventually became a physically imposing big man in the league.

On the offensive end, Davis seemed like he could still improve to become not only a great finisher but also a phenomenal scorer. Adding a few pounds to his frame helped him become a better post player against the stronger NBA defenders. While he did not have a consistent jump shot back in college, his form always looked pleasing, and it seemed like he had the makings of a big man who could stretch the floor with his shooting. Because he grew up knowing how to handle the ball, Davis could develop into a fearsome player who could take slower big men off the dribble to create shots for himself or his teammates.

Anthony Davis also showed a great understanding of the game, not only when he was protecting the basket but also when he was asked to make plays. Though he was not Kentucky's top playmaker, Davis showed flashes of his high basketball IQ by making smart passes and executing plays almost to perfection. He never did more than what was necessary, and it always seemed like he knew what was happening on the floor. This was a reason why he had an extremely low turnover rate in college.

With all that said and done, Anthony Davis was all potential, not only because of his rare physical gifts but also because he had a unique, innate understanding of the game that not many big men had. Nobody else was skilled enough to take that top spot away from him.

To his credit, Davis never showed many weaknesses to make scouts and teams feel like he was not deserving of the number one overall pick. While he was still a work in progress when it came down to his ability to produce points, what was obvious was that he was already prepared to deliver on the defensive end.

Knowing how much talent and potential Anthony Davis had in his skinny 6'10" frame, there was no reason for the New Orleans Hornets to shy away from taking him with the top overall pick of that year's draft. Taking Davis meant that they could speed up their rebuilding process just a season after they had traded Chris Paul away to the Los Angeles Clippers. It also meant that they had a new face for the franchise to build on for the future. After his fellow Kentucky standout Michael Kidd-Gilchrist was selected with the second overall pick, Davis and MKG became the first pair of teammates to be in the top two picks in the same draft class. However, even before Davis could make his NBA debut, he was already making a big splash in the international scene.

During the summer of 2012, Davis got the chance to play with the NBA's best against the best of the world. In the Summer Olympics in London, Davis was chosen to join forces with a superstar team consisting of LeBron James, Kobe Bryant, Kevin Durant, Chris Paul, and many more elite-level players. Even before Davis ever started playing professionally, Kevin Love claimed that, within the next two years, Davis would pose a threat in the NBA. Davis received mentorship from Kobe and LeBron throughout their Olympic journey, and the experience undoubtedly helped prepare him to become the player he is today.

To be able to play and learn from the best was an excellent opportunity for Anthony. How often do you get to learn from several MVP-caliber players from the NBA? Davis absorbed all the knowledge that he could during their championship run. He started his NBA career with a gold medal at the

Olympics and an NCAA title, giving him all the confidence in the world. And he achieved all of that even before he played his first NBA game.

Rookie Year

After helping Team USA win gold in the Olympics, Anthony Davis was set to join a rebuilding New Orleans Hornets franchise that was still moving on from the Chris Paul era. They were a relatively young team with the likes of Eric Gordon, Robin Lopez, Ryan Anderson, Greivis Vasquez, and Al-Farouq Aminu still developing at the early stages of their respective careers. Davis also came in with a highly-touted rookie guard, Austin Rivers, whom everybody thought would pair up with him to form a young inside-outside tandem.

With Davis on a high after tasting an NCAA title and a gold medal in the same year, he had all the confidence in the world to try to make a big splash in the NBA and to try to lead the New Orleans Hornets back to relevance in his rookie season as a professional player. However, he soon realized that things were not going to be as easy as they were in college.

On October 31, 2012, Anthony Davis made his NBA debut against a then-underrated powerhouse team, the San Antonio Spurs. He was going up against none other than Tim Duncan, who has spent a legendary, successful career in the NBA. In this game, Davis posted 21 points, 7 rebounds, and a block. He made 50% percent of his shots from the field and all nine of his free throws. However, his team failed to take the win as they fell to the better team. He also struggled against their experienced star, as Tim Duncan had 24 points and 11 rebounds in the game.

Overall, Davis had a topsy-turvy transition into the NBA. The next game, he went on to score only eight points in 14 minutes of play in a win over the

35

Utah Jazz. Although he was an unusually talented athlete, the game in the NBA was different. It was much faster, and there were guys who were considerably larger than Davis. Moreover, an NBA season was a lot longer than it was at the college level, so everything was taking a toll on him. So, as with many players making the transition from college to the pros, there was still a period of adjustment for the big-man Kentucky product, and he had to deal with a few injuries in his first season as well.

After sitting out a few games because of a concussion he suffered against the Jazz, he made his return on November 9th. In this game, he posted his first double-double with 23 points and 11 rebounds to go along with 2 assists, 2 steals, and 6 blocks. That game was an omen of how dominant Davis would be in the future. The Hornets won that game by eight points. After that, a few more tough losses followed. Davis scored eight points in a losing effort against the Houston Rockets on November 14th, and another eight points against the Oklahoma City Thunder on November 15th. However, he had a big game with 28 points and 11 rebounds after shooting 10 out of 13 from the field in a loss to the Bucks on November 17th.

Despite Davis coming back strong, he then suffered a second injury that required him to miss more time. He had a stress reaction in his ankle and was forced to miss 11 games before eventually returning to face the Washington Wizards in a disappointing loss on December 11th. Without Anthony Davis, the New Orleans Hornets won only 2 out of those 11 games.

In his return game, Davis came off the bench and made 5 out of 10 field goals and all 3 free throws for 13 total points to go along with 8 rebounds, 3 steals, and 3 blocked shots. In their next game on December 12th, Davis struggled while making only 3 out of 8 from the field to score 11 points off the bench with 4 rebounds in a 92-88 loss at Oklahoma City. He continued to score in double figures as his minutes increased.

Davis returned to the starting lineup on December 18th, on the road against the Golden State Warriors in Oakland, California, where he collected a then-career-high 16 rebounds to go along with 15 points. As the losses continued to pile up, the realization was that the Hornets were not a competitive team that season. While Davis had plenty of talent and potential, there was only so much he could do. Not many teams can make the transition from being a notably bad team to being a playoff contender simply after drafting a top overall pick, and the Hornets were no exception. Yet, on the bright side, they had a talented big man to build their team around.

Davis and the Hornets were on an 11-game losing streak before finally getting a win over the Orlando Magic on December 25th, where he had 27 points, 8 assists, 6 rebounds, and a steal in about 33 and a half minutes in that win. During that losing streak, Davis's playing time was increasing. While he averaged decent numbers for a rookie, it was not the same dominating stats that fans were accustomed to seeing from him during his days in Kentucky.

Nevertheless, Anthony Davis improved throughout the season, just as most rookies do. It was evident to the NBA that Davis was not there just yet concerning his peak, but he was clearly moving in the right direction and showing tantalizing glimpses of his future potential. He had to improve and develop his offensive game and gain a little more muscle to become a force with which to be reckoned. He was often compared to Marcus Camby and Lamar Odom. Both players were productive and versatile at the defensive end, but Odom had playmaking abilities and was a decent jumper whereas Anthony Davis was yet to develop that part of his game.

His season, however, was cut short after being diagnosed with an MCL sprain and bone bruising. The Hornets decided to exercise caution with their investment and expected Davis to come back the following year better and healthier. Therefore, he finished his season with three games still left to play in April. The Hornets finished the season with a 27-55 record and last place in the Southwest Division of the Western Conference.

A Rising Star

As the New Year came roaring in, so did Anthony Davis, as he saw himself winning several games in a row for the first time in his pro career. On January 5, 2013, he only played 12 minutes but helped his team win against the Dallas Mavericks. He then followed that up with 17 points and 9 rebounds in a win over a powerhouse San Antonio Spurs team. Despite combining to score only 15 points in the next two games, Davis helped the Hornets win against the Houston Rockets and the Minnesota Timberwolves.

After a few mediocre games for Anthony Davis, he went for an excellent double-double output on January 19th. In that loss to the Golden State Warriors, he had 20 points, 12 rebounds, 4 assists, and 4 blocks. Despite that loss, he filled up the stat sheet and shot 9 out of 12 from the floor. That was only a game after he struggled for a double-double in a win over the Boston Celtics.

On February 13th, just before the All-Star Weekend, Davis went for another 20-10 game. Helping his New Orleans Hornets in that 36-point blowout win over the Portland Trail Blazers, he had 21 points, 11 rebounds, and 2 blocks while playing only about 28 minutes that night. That was all the momentum Davis needed on his way to his first appearance at the All-Star Weekend. During the midseason festivities, Davis helped Team Chuck win against

Team Shaq in the Rising Stars Challenge. He went for 11 points, 9 rebounds, and 2 blocks in that game.

Anthony Davis went for a new career high in rebounds on March 9th. In that loss to the Memphis Grizzlies, Davis banged bodies against a hefty frontline to go for 18 rebounds on top of the 20 points he scored. Despite that loss, Davis carried the momentum to secure two more double-double performances in a win over Portland and a loss to the Brooklyn Nets in the next two games.

But just when Davis was averaging 16 points and 9 rebounds in his last 10 games, he suffered another injury. On April 10th, against the Sacramento Kings, he suffered an MCL sprain and a bone bruise after he collided with Marcus Thornton. His season abruptly ended because of that injury, and the Hornets had to shut him down without any hopes of making it to the postseason.

After averaging 13.5 points, 8.2 rebounds, and nearly 2 blocks per game, he ended up as the runner-up for the Rookie of the Year behind Damian Lillard, who played for the Portland Trail Blazers. Lillard had per-game averages of 19 points, 6.5 assists, and 3.1 rebounds while shooting 42.9% from the field. Despite being the runner-up, Davis was still named to the NBA All-Rookie first team.

Even though Davis did not have the best rookie season, there were already clear flashes of what kind of player he could be. He showcased his incredible mobility and athleticism at the power forward spot early in his career. But the best part was that he was already quite versatile as a rookie after showing that he could handle the ball, keep up with smaller offensive players, and hit the occasional jumper.

At the same time, however, what was also clear was that he struggled to keep up with the physicality of the bigger players in the league. AD may have been athletic and talented but he did not have the heft and strength that allowed him to bang bodies with bigger power forwards and centers inside the paint. So, if he wanted to be the best version of himself, he needed to put on some muscle mass without necessarily slowing his body down. That was the long-term project that Davis needed to accomplish during the earlier part of his career.

Before the start of the 2013-2014 NBA season, changes were made to the team. These changes started back in December 2012 when the new team owner, Tom Benson, wanted to change the team's name to something that was more local than Hornets. The organization then changed its name to "Pelicans" to represent Louisiana's state bird, the brown pelican.

The name change was followed by the release of a color scheme with blue, gold, and red and a new logo in the final months of Davis's rookie season. The Hornets officially became the Pelicans the day after their season ended on April 18, 2013. This followed quickly after Michael Jordan, owner of the Charlotte NBA team, brought the Hornets back to North Carolina.

The name change came at an opportune time for the New Orleans franchise. The Pelicans moniker was befitting of how they found a new face that could help the franchise fly as high as he could. Despite not making the big splash that everyone thought he would in his rookie season, Anthony Davis showed flashes of brilliance, especially during the final stages of his first year in the NBA. For some, it was only a matter of time before he became a legitimate star in the league.

There was a good reason to believe he was going to be a star. Davis was an incredible specimen in his rookie season not because of his unibrow or physical measurements. What made him such a promising rookie was how impressively productive he was, even in the limited role he was given. Out of all the players in the league, Davis was the only one who had a player efficiency rating (PER) that was over 21 but with a usage rate of under 22%. What that meant was that Anthony Davis could produce with so little.

Just like in college, Davis had one of the best turnover rates in the entire league in his rookie season. He only turned the ball over about 10% of his possessions. Davis had a fantastic basketball IQ, reflected by the fact that he never did *too* much of what was asked of him. He knew his capacity as a player and stuck with what he knew he could do well. He let the game come to him instead of trying to do too much to the detriment of his team.

One way that Davis showcased his unique talent as a player who only made the most efficient shots was how he finished transition baskets. He was never the fastest player, but his long strides and incredible mobility for his size helped him run the break faster than any other big man. Using his body control and soft hands in transition, he was always in rhythm for the best possible finish at the rim. Because of that, he was second in the entire league concerning points per possession in transition, meaning that he almost always finished his baskets in transition.[ii]

Because he was far ahead of other big men concerning mobility and athleticism, Davis was already a tremendous pick-and-roll option for New Orleans. During pick-and-roll situations, he could finish 56% of his attempts and ranked 33 in the NBA when it came to points scored on the pick-and-roll. Plus, Davis could do this with mediocre guards Greivis Vasquez and Austin Rivers running the pick-and-roll for him.

While some point out Davis's superior mobility and body control as the primary reason why he was such a good pick-and-roll player, what was even more crucial was his basketball IQ. He never tried to force the issue on the pick-and-roll because he always surveyed the floor first before trying to run the play. He already showed a strong sense of knowing when to slip and drive to the basket by viewing and carefully assessing the area around him and the paint.[ii]

After spending much of his college career as an off-the-ball scorer, Anthony Davis was also a terrific cutter in his rookie season in the NBA. When not playing the pick-and-roll or putting back offensive rebounds, Davis knew how to space the floor and cut to the basket by knowing where he should be and where his teammates were. He rarely clogged the basket and only ran to the paint whenever he saw that his teammates could get him an open look near the rim. Frankly, it was incredible for Davis to do so much with the limited possessions and plays that were called for him as a rookie.

However, with opposing teams now looking to focus their defense more on Davis, Davis needed more than just pick-and-roll finishes, offensive putbacks, and cuts to help his team on the offensive end. What he needed was to be able to generate points for himself without the help of his teammates. One way for him to do that was to learn how to score from the post, which was a particular area of weakness due to his slight build and lack of strength.[ii] Thus, if Davis wanted to take his game to the next level, he needed to bulk up and improve his strength during the offseason.

First All-Star Season

After that underwhelming but still highly promising rookie season for Anthony Davis, there was already speculation that he would take a rising star

42

role for the New Orleans Pelicans in his next season. There was no argument that he was already a productive player in just his rookie season. However, the consensus was that he needed to learn how to create shots to become a true star in the league.

During the offseason, there was a noticeable difference in Anthony Davis's physique. Listed at 220 pounds during his rookie year, he admitted that he packed on at least 10 more pounds of muscle during the offseason by eating more and getting into the weight room. One knock on his game during his rookie season was that his speed and mobility were offset by his lack of strength to bang with opposing big men. With Davis getting stronger, there was a reason to believe he was more equipped to score down at the low post and contain other big men on the defensive end.[iii]

Adding strength and weight meant that the young power forward could also play the center position. The Pelicans just recently lost starting center Robin Lopez, meaning that they were a little thin at the center spot. But with Davis becoming stronger and more muscular, he could play the center spot on certain occasions to become a matchup nightmare because of his quickness. With him at the center spot, the New Orleans Pelicans could mix their offense up by putting Ryan Anderson, who had spent the last season as Davis's backup, at the power forward spot to add more dimension and spacing on the floor.[iii]

The added muscle was not the only reason why experts believed Davis was ready to become a star. It was his unique offense that made scouts believe he had the potential to do something great in the NBA. Anthony Davis was like Lamar Odom in the sense that he had the ball-handling skills and mobility of a guard despite standing at about 6'10".[iii] But Davis was always more agile and athletic than Odom. Add to that the fact that he was already trying to

43

develop his jump shot, and there was a reason to believe that Anthony Davis was going to become a scary offensive weapon for the New Orleans Pelicans.

Offense is not always the reason why a player is considered a star. As the old saying goes, offense sells tickets, but defense wins championships. Clearly, the best teams in the NBA demonstrate adeptness at both ends of the floor, but many great defenders have made considerable differences in the NBA just with their defensive skills.

In Anthony Davis's case, his defensive abilities only improved with the experience he got in his rookie year. While his offense was predicted to grow in time, he already had the tools necessary to become an elite defensive force in the NBA. Davis was not only a fantastic rim protector for the Pelicans but was also one of the best big men at playing the passing lanes. Using his long arms, he not only blocked shots but also disrupted passes for steals and deflections. With Davis becoming a more stable post defender with the added strength, he was going to be a much better defensive player than he already was in his rookie year. And Anthony Davis with an improved offense output and defensive capability meant instant stardom for the sophomore professional player.

With Davis predicted to become an improved two-way star in the league, there was a reason to believe that the New Orleans Pelicans were ready to take it to the next level in the maiden year of their new moniker. Luckily for Davis, the personnel around him also improved. The team added 2013 All-Star player Jrue Holiday in an offseason trade for their 2013 draft pick, Nerlens Noel. Holiday was a noticeable upgrade to the slower but bigger Greivis Vasquez. The Pelicans, wanting to add more dimension to their offense, brought in 2010 Rookie of the Year Tyreke Evans, who was known for his slashing and playmaking skills at the wing. Adding more talent to the roster meant that Davis had more room to operate inside the basket.

Proving that he was ready to take his game to the next level, Anthony Davis started the season strong. On October 30, 2013, he went for 20 points, 12 rebounds, and 3 blocks in a narrow loss to the Indiana Pacers. After that solid outing, he went to Orlando two days later to finish a loss with 26 points, 17 rebounds, and 3 blocks.

Anthony Davis led the Pelicans to their first win of the season on November 2nd against the Charlotte Bobcats. It was in that game when Davis showed his ability to produce at an elite rate across the board. He finished the game with 26 points, 8 rebounds, 4 assists, 6 steals, and 6 blocks. He became the first player in two decades to have 25 points, 6 steals, and 6 blocks in one game. That stat line alone showed how Davis was prepared to produce at an elite level on both ends of the floor.

On November 8th, Davis took his offense to the next level by going for a new career high in points. While making 12 of his 18 attempts from the floor, Davis finished a win over the LA Lakers with 32 points on top of the 12 rebounds and 6 blocks he recorded that night. With that performance at the age of 20, Davis became the youngest person to record at least 30 points, 10 rebounds, and 5 blocks in a single game.

Anthony Davis led his team to a significant 37-point blowout win over the Philadelphia 76ers on November 15th by playing his best brand of defense. While he finished the game with 13 points and 9 rebounds, Davis made his mark on the defensive end by blocking 9 shots. Four days later, he played a similar brand of basketball. In that win against the Utah Jazz, Davis had 22 points, 9 rebounds, 4 assists, and 8 blocks. With those performances, he became just the second player since Roy Hibbert to have at least eight blocks in at least two games in a season. To date, nobody has replicated that feat since.

Just when he was averaging 16 points, 9.7 rebounds, and 5 blocks in the last six games, Anthony Davis hit a roadblock early in the season. He suffered a fracture in his left hand after trying to draw a charge against Amar'e Stoudemire in a game against the New York Knicks on December 1st. He only played 10 minutes before leaving the game because of that injury.

While the initial prediction was that he would miss at least four weeks, Davis made a comeback in only a little over two weeks. Davis missed a total of seven games, wherein the Pelicans went 2-5. He made his return on December 18th in a loss to the Los Angeles Clippers. In that game, Davis finished with 24 points, 12 rebounds, and 3 steals in 32 minutes off the bench. It did not seem like he missed a beat as he scored at least 20 points in the next two games.

On January 7, 2014, Anthony Davis began a personal best of eight consecutive games of scoring at least 20 points. He started by going for 22 points, 12 rebounds, 3 steals, and 2 blocks in a loss to the Miami Heat, who were the defending champions that season. After scoring 21 in the next two games, he went for 28 points and 14 rebounds in a three-point loss to the Dallas Mavericks on January 11th.

Davis scored at least 20 points in his seventh consecutive game on January 18th. In that loss to the Golden State Warriors, he had 31 points and 17 rebounds. And two days later, he finished his eight-game streak with 27 points, 10 rebounds, 4 steals, and 4 blocks. Despite that personal-best streak, the Pelicans were 1-7 during that stretch of games. Davis averaged 24.5

points, 11.4 rebounds, 1.9 steals, and 2.3 blocks during that personal eight-game run.

On January 25th, Davis had another fantastic outing in a win against the Orlando Magic. While his 22 points were not very impressive, he grabbed a career-high 19 rebounds and also finished the game with 7 blocks. Two days later in a win over the Cleveland Cavaliers, Davis also had another tremendous overall outing by going for 30 points, 7 rebounds, and 8 blocks. That was the third time he had eight blocks in a game that season.

After missing a game due to a dislocated finger, Anthony Davis immediately went back to work by going for 24 points, 8 rebounds, 3 assists, 3 steals, and six blocks in a win over the Chicago Bulls. Then, on February 3rd, he went for 17 points, 16 rebounds, and 4 blocks to mark the seventh consecutive game in which he blocked at least 4 shots. During those seven games, he averaged 21.4 points, 10.6 rebounds, and 5.3 blocks.

Davis was selected to take part in the Rising Stars Challenge but was initially left off the Western All-Stars' roster. However, he was later named an All-Star after Kobe Bryant was unable to participate in the event due to injury. Davis was named the Black Mamba's replacement. He went for 10 points in only 9 minutes of play in the midseason classic, which the Western All-Stars won.

On a high just a few days after making his first All-Star appearance, Davis went for 32 points on 14 out of 18 shooting from the field in a loss to the Phoenix Suns on February 28th. After scoring 32 points that night, Davis tied his career-high in points. Yet that was not his best scoring output that season, and he later broke that personal record.

On March 9th, Davis once again tied his career high in points. In that win over the Denver Nuggets, he had an excellent outing after going for 32 points, 17 rebounds, 3 assists, and 6 blocks. Five days later, he broke that career high by going for 36 points on 15 out of 27 shooting in a loss to the Portland Trail Blazers. However, that was far from his best performance that season.

On March 15th, Anthony Davis made history by becoming the youngest player in over 20 years to record at least 40 points and 20 rebounds in a single game. In that overtime win against the Boston Celtics, Davis made 14 of his 22 shots from the floor to score 40 points. He also had 21 rebounds to record his first 40-20 game. At 21 years old, he was the youngest player to do it since Shaquille O'Neal accomplished the feat in 1993.

Just five days later, he had another fantastic game by going for 34 points and 11 rebounds in a win over the Atlanta Hawks. He then led the way to a win over the powerhouse Miami Heat team a night later with 30 points and 11 rebounds. That performance marked the fourth consecutive 30-point game for Davis. He averaged an incredible 35 points and 13 rebounds during that stretch.

However, similar to the previous season, Davis suffered injuries that prematurely ended his season. A left ankle sprain late in March and back spasms early in April forced the New Orleans Pelicans to leave him off the lineup in the team's final five games. It was a safe decision for the franchise, considering that they were already well out of playoff contention.

After another injury-prone season, the first-time All-Star averaged 20.8 points, 10 rebounds, 1.6 steals, and 2.8 blocks in the 67 games he played. He finished the season with improved overall numbers from across the board. While his scoring increased, his field-goal shooting and free-throw percentages also improved despite taking and attempting more shots. He also led the league in blocks per game that season. Because of his improved stats, Anthony Davis was one of the most improved players in the league and finished behind Goran Dragić and Lance Stephenson for the Most Improved Player Award. However, the Pelicans only improved slightly after winning just 34 games that season.

Nevertheless, there were plenty of reasons to be hopeful about the New Orleans Pelicans, primarily because of Anthony Davis's growth. From a college standout coveted because he could defend at an elite level, rebound the ball well, and finish around the basket at a high rate, his offense evolved to the point where he could generate shots for himself inside the paint.

It also helped that Davis has learned how to take his game away from the basket. During his rookie year, 47% of his shots came from within three feet away from the basket. He had initially struggled to create for himself, as 76.5% of his scoring was assisted. However, he learned how to generate points for himself in his second year in the NBA. Only 66.7% of his shots were assisted while he learned how to manufacture shots a little farther away from the basket. He only took 39.6% of his shots from within three feet of the basket and began shooting more from mid-range. He made 40% of his mid-range shots in his first All-Star season after making only 29% of those attempts back when he was still a rookie.

Davis's improvement as a mid-range shooter that season was only secondary to how well he had bulked up his physique to bang with opposing big men, not only on the offensive end but the defensive part of the floor as well. While his post scoring improved because of his added strength, he also developed into an even better defender because of how well he could take the pounding and beating inside. Because of that, he led the league in blocks per game while also finishing the season as one of the best big men when it came to stealing the ball.

Experts had been right about Anthony Davis's growth as a star that season. However, the 21-year-old power forward still had a long way to go, and he was only scratching the surface of his vast potential. He may have already been an All-Star, but he was still developing into one of the most elite players in the entire NBA. Still, nobody expected him to do it as early as his third season in the league.

Rise to Elite Status, Playoff Debut

After making the All-Star team for the first time, Davis still had a long way to go in his young career. The 21-year-old big man was considered one of the league's brightest stars and still had great potential and room to grow. From a physical standpoint, Davis began to work on developing into his frame. It turned out that the added strength and muscle had helped him a lot in the last season, and it inspired him to keep working on it.

During the offseason, Davis packed eight more pounds of lean muscle mass onto his body. One of his goals during the break was to become stronger so that it became easier for him to post down low. More importantly, the knowledge that he had grown stronger also helped his mentality and aggressiveness out on the floor, as he now knew that it would be harder for opposing big men to push him out of his position. Measured at 6'10" when he was still a 19-year-old rookie, Anthony Davis even thought that he had grown about an inch.[iv] He was still listed at 6'10" despite the fact that he did grow a bit taller. But he was now nearly 240 pounds. Thus, Anthony Davis was becoming an even scarier big man than he already was.

Not content with the added strength, Anthony thought that he still had room to grow as an offensive player as well. One particular part of his game that he worked on during the offseason was his shooting. Davis spent time trying to develop his jump shot and even worked on his three-point shooting from the corner. He had only made two three-pointers in the last two years, but the added dimension to his offense made him a more efficient scorer from the rest of the floor, especially considering that he was also working on his post moves and his dribbles during the offseason.[iv]

While Davis tried to dismiss his drastic improvement from his rookie season to his second year as merely a product of his growing confidence, the numbers showed that it was more than that. However, he also understood that it took more than confidence to make the jump to an elite level in his third year in the NBA.[iv] Because of that, it was necessary for him to get better from an all-around standpoint. That included his health and leadership as he hoped to take his team to the playoffs in just his third year in the NBA.

As the New Orleans Pelicans were looking to make a splash during the 2014-15 season, they retained the core group that helped them improve their record last season while adding center Omer Asik to help Davis on the frontlines. With that, head coach Monty Williams was hopeful that he and the rest of the Pelicans could contend for a playoff spot with the group they had that season.

When the 2014-15 season started, Anthony Davis immediately showed how much he had improved. On October 28, 2014, he opened the season with a statement win over the Orlando Magic by putting up 26 points, 17 rebounds, 3 steals, and 9 blocks. It was one of the best opening performances in league history, as Davis was the first to have at least nine blocks in an opening game. The last person to do that was Nate Thurmond back in 1974. Davis also became the first player to have that stat line since Hakeem Olajuwon did it during the 1989-90 season. At such a young age, he was already doing things that only the league's most legendary players could do.

Anthony Davis rode the high of a strong opening performance by scoring at least 20 points in 9 of his first 10 games. During that 10-game span, he averaged 25.5 points, 11.4 rebounds, 2.3 steals, and 3.9 blocks while shooting 58% from the floor. More importantly, the Pelicans only lost 3 of those first 10 games to start the season strong.

After that strong 10-game start, Anthony Davis never relented. He had one of his best games at that point of the season on November 22nd against the Utah Jazz. In that game, he made 16 of his 23 shots from the floor and 11 of his 12 free throws to score a new career high of 43 points. He also had 14 rebounds in that win over the Jazz.

Showing that he was indeed a player who could fill the stat sheet up in all of the game's facets, Davis nearly became the youngest player to record a five-by-five, which was recording at least five in all of the game's five major statistical categories. In that win over the Oklahoma City Thunder, Anthony Davis finished with 35 points, 10 rebounds, 4 assists, 6 steals, and 4 blocks. He was just an assist and a block shy of that elusive five-by-five.

After playing 21 games that season, Davis was averaging 25.1 points, 10.6 rebounds, 2.0 steals, and 2.9 blocks. He was also shooting 57% from the floor and 77.5% from the free-throw line. Because of that, he was coming into his 22nd game of the season with a PER of 32.9, which would have been an all-time high for the NBA if he had maintained it all season long. While he did not do that, there was no denying that Davis was already showing that he was an elite and efficient player early in the season.

Davis missed a game because of an injury he sustained against the Cleveland Cavaliers on December 12th. He came back after one missed game and continued to put up dominant numbers. On December 15th, he had 31 points and 9 rebounds in a win over the Utah Jazz. Two days later, he went for 30 points, 14 rebounds, 2 steals, and 5 blocks in a win against the Houston Rockets.

After a dismal 3 of 14 shooting from the field in a loss to the Portland Trail Blazers on December 20th, Davis bounced back with an excellent performance in a win over the OKC Thunder just a day later. In that game, he made 16 of his 22 shots to score 38 points while also finishing the game with 12 rebounds and 3 blocks.

On January 5, 2015, Anthony Davis began mounting what eventually became a 13-game streak of consecutive 20-point performances. It started with an underwhelming loss to the Washington Wizards. Davis only had 21 points and 10 rebounds that night. He then had 32 points and 12 rebounds two days later in a loss to the Charlotte Hornets.

After going for 34 and 27 points respectively against the Boston Celtics and Detroit Pistons, Davis missed three games because of an injury. He returned on January 21st in a win versus the Los Angeles Lakers to score 29 points in addition to having 3 steals and 4 blocks. He then continued his streak of consecutive 20-point scoring performances.

On February 5th, Davis punctuated his 13-game streak by going for another 40-point output that season. In that win over the OKC Thunder, the Pelicans' superstar made 15 of his 23 shots from the floor and all 10 of his free throws to score 41 points in addition to having 10 rebounds, 2 steals, and 3 blocks.

He also made a buzzer-beating three-pointer to win the game for the New Orleans Pelicans.

After playing nine minutes in a win over the Miami Heat on February 7th, Anthony left the game because of a shoulder injury. He only scored 6 points, and his 13-game streak of consecutive 20-point games came to an end. Nevertheless, Davis surpassed Pete Maravich in that regard and became the franchise leader in straight games of scoring at least 20 points.

While Anthony Davis may have been voted in by fans as a starter for the Western All-Star squad after barely making it onto the team the last season, he was forced to sit out of that event because of the shoulder injury he had sustained in that game against the Heat. Dirk Nowitzki was named his replacement for the event while LaMarcus Aldridge was named the starter in his place.

Though Davis returned on February 20th, it was evident that he was still hobbled by the injury. In the two games he played immediately after returning, he shot 7 out of 23 for a total of only 19 points. Because it was evident that he was still feeling the effects of the injured shoulder, Davis was forced to sit out a few more games until he was back to full health.

Anthony Davis made his triumphant return on March 4th. In a win over the Detroit Pistons, Davis dominated in a way that only Hakeem Olajuwon and Dwight Howard have done in the last 30 years. Davis, finally feeling healthy, made 17 of his 30 shots to score 39 points while also finishing the game with 13 rebounds, 3 steals, and 8 blocks. Only Olajuwon and Howard have had at least 39 points, 13 rebounds, and 8 blocks in a single game over the last three decades.

Five days after that dominant performance against the Pistons, Davis had another monster game at the expense of the Milwaukee Bucks. Making 17 of his 23 shots, Davis tied his career high of 43 points while also collecting 10 rebounds, 6 assists, 2 steals, and 4 blocks in that win over Milwaukee. However, that was not the end of his stat-stuffing days that season.

On March 15th, in an overtime loss to the Denver Nuggets, Davis made history yet again by becoming the only player in league history to have at least 36 points, 7 assists, and 9 blocks since the NBA officially started to count blocks in 1973. The only player even close to what Davis achieved was David Robinson. Davis also collected 14 rebounds in that monstrous performance for the third-year power forward.

Since coming back from his shoulder injury, Anthony was nothing short of dominant. He was averaging 30.8 points, 11.2 rebounds, 3.8 assists, and 5 blocks in the first 6 games he played since his return. While he could not sustain such a phenomenal stat line through the end of the season, he still put up impressive numbers while leading the New Orleans Pelicans to an 8-5 record in their last 13 games.

At the end of such a successful regular season for Anthony Davis, there was no denying that he had already reached superstardom in only his third year in the NBA. Davis averaged 24.4 points, 10.2 rebounds, 2.2 assists, 1.5 steals, and a league-leading 2.9 blocks the entire season. He also shot an improved 53.5% from the floor and 80.5% from the free-throw line. For the second consecutive year, Anthony Davis's numbers improved across the board.

Davis also ended the season with a player efficiency rating of 30.8, which was the best in the NBA that season, and one of the best in league history. His PER that season ranked as one of the best. At that time, it was the 11th highest before Stephen Curry overtook him the following season. His PER that season had already decreased in terms of its rankings with the emergence of new players who were able to have incredibly efficient seasons. But the fact that Davis did that in just his third season in the league was a testament to his talent and deep potential. With such a high PER, Anthony Davis had already crossed borders that only the most elite players in the league will ever cross. And not even some of the greatest names in league history were able to reach a PER of 30 at least once in their careers.

Even though Davis was not named the MVP of the league that season, he had a higher PER than Stephen Curry, James Harden, and LeBron James, who were the top three finishers in terms of votes for that award. Though Davis finished fifth in the MVP voting, he was still named to an All-NBA first team after such a historic season, and after leading the Pelicans to a 45-37 record, which was good enough for the eighth seed in the West. With that, Davis was on his way to the playoffs for the first time in his career.

The Pelicans found themselves facing off against the top-seeded Golden State Warriors, a team that featured the formidable core of Stephen Curry, Klay Thompson, and Draymond Green. However, Davis did not want to be intimidated by a team that had finished the regular season with 67 wins and only 15 losses. The Pelicans were going to have their work cut out for them.

The first game of the Western Conference first-round series took place on April 18th at the Oracle Arena in Oakland, Davis led New Orleans with 35 points after shooting 13 out of 23 for a 56.5 field-goal percentage and converted 9 out of 10 free throws during the team's loss. Davis also had seven rebounds and four blocked shots.

The Pelicans continued to struggle as a team in the second game of the series on April 20th, and the Warriors took a 2-0 lead in the series. New Orleans had a team shooting percentage of only 38.3% from the field because of the stifling Warriors defense. Davis only made 9 out of his 22 field goals but made all 8 free throws. He led the team with 26 points along with 11 rebounds, 3 assists, 2 steals, and 2 blocked shots.

The series then went back to New Orleans, and the hometown crowd helped the Pelicans build a 20-point lead entering the third quarter. However, the Warriors outscored New Orleans 39-19 to send the game into overtime via a Steph Curry three-pointer at the end of the fourth quarter. The Warriors eventually won, gaining a 3-0 series lead. After Davis scored 11 points in the first quarter, he finished with 29 points, 15 rebounds, 3 blocks, 3 assists, and 2 steals while making 11 out of 22 from the field and 7 of 9 free throws.

This was a tight spot for any NBA team to be in because not many teams were able to bounce back after being down 3-0. Every professional sport that uses the best-of-seven format rarely sees anyone come back from that daunting deficit.

The Pelicans tried valiantly to fight it out. However, they found themselves trailing by 20 points entering the fourth quarter in Game 4. They were only able to make up 10 points in the difference before their season ended with a loss to give the Warriors a first-round sweep.

The Warriors squad had impressive scoring with Curry taking the lead with 39 points. Still, Davis never gave up. He had one of his best efforts in the series with a final line of 36 points, 11 rebounds, and 3 blocked shots. He was also quite efficient, making 14 out of 20 of his shots from the field. The Warriors just outplayed them, plain and simple. They were an iconic team that eventually won the entire playoffs and were crowned the 2015 NBA Champions.

Despite an early exit for Anthony Davis and the rest of the New Orleans Pelicans, what was clear to the rest of the world was that Davis had already begun to scratch the surface of the potential that had gotten the NBA excited about him back in 2012. His talent was undeniable and his efficiency on both ends of the floor was nearly unmatched in the league. He was becoming the league's premier two-way big man. No other power forward or center in the entire NBA could match what he could do on both ends of the floor. What was more impressive was how quickly Davis made the jump to superstardom.

Back in 2012, scouts reported that Davis had trouble with manufacturing his own shots. He rarely dribbled the ball or even shot beyond five feet away from the basket. Davis was then more of a finisher who relied more on his teammates to give him open looks near the basket. There was no doubt that he was an excellent finisher when he got close to the basket. However, the consensus at that time was for defenses to make him work for his points by pushing him out of the paint or by making him put the ball on the floor.

Nobody had expected how big of a jump Davis would make from being a finisher in 2012 to an elite scoring presence during the 2014-15 season. While some attributed his improved inside and low-post scoring to his added strength and bulk along with his developing post-game, his jump shot ultimately made the difference for him and his offense.

After spending much of his time taking close shots during his first two seasons, Davis began shooting more from beyond the 15-foot line in his third season. He only attempted about 21% of his shots from 16 feet and beyond in his second year but increased that to 29% in his third season. After

58

shooting just 37% from that area the previous season, his percentage from that distance shot up to 42% during the 2014-15 season.

The numbers showed that Davis had begun to rely more on his mid-range game rather than waiting inside the paint for drop passes and lobs. He was making himself an even harder player to guard because of the range that he added to his game. Even though he was shooting more mid-range jumpers than he ever did at that point in his career, his efficiency from the field improved. Defenses became wary of his ability to finish near the basket and dared him to shoot from the perimeter, as scouts said back in 2012. However, this only gave him room to operate outside of the paint. If defenses adjusted to his improved jumper, Anthony Davis was skilled enough to take his man off the dribble and finish strong at the rim.

At 22 years old, Davis had already turned himself into an impossible-to-guard superstar because of how he improved his mid-range game. Many expected him to improve his jumper but nobody thought he would turn out to become one of the best in the league at hitting mid-range shots. Davis ranked 10th in the league in field-goal percentage from 15 to 19 feet away from the basket, and 12th from 10 to 14 feet. As a 6'11" power forward, he was shooting the mid-range jumper better than even the best guards in the NBA. This was not just a product of his height, length, and vertical leaping ability. Confidence also played a factor, but it all boiled down to how hard Davis had worked on his jumper during the offseason.

Given his young age, Anthony Davis still had significant room for improvement left. He was already arguably just as difficult to guard as the likes of Dirk Nowitzki and Kevin Garnett in their respective primes because of his efficient mid-range game and the way he could take his defenders off the dribble whenever they decided to respect his jumper.

However, if Davis could add a consistent three-point shot to his game like Dirk did, there was no telling how far he could take his offense. At that point, probably the only player in the NBA who was considered more difficult to guard than Davis was Kevin Durant. If Davis could learn how to shoot long shots with efficiency, not even Durant could hold a candle to Davis's unique offensive skillset.

Plagued by Injuries

Just after the 2014-15 season ended, the New Orleans Pelicans replaced Monty Williams with Alvin Gentry, who was an assistant for Steve Kerr during the Warriors' 2015 title run. Gentry was known for his successful stint with the Phoenix Suns a few years earlier when he blended their running style with a defensive mindset. He also helped the Warriors develop a smooth and fast-paced offense during the 2014-15 season.

However, now the head coach of the Pelicans, Gentry saw what Anthony Davis could do as an offensive player during the first-round matchup between Golden State and New Orleans. After seeing how great of a player Davis was, he knew that he had a gem in the 22-year-old power forward, and planned to make him a more significant focal point on the offensive end. He even went as far as saying that he would "unleash" Anthony Davis because of how he planned to have the Pelicans play a faster pace of basketball.[v] Because of that, the whole world was excited about how far Davis improved as an offensive player for New Orleans.

In Anthony Davis's case, it was going to be an entirely new adjustment period for him to be playing for Alvin Gentry's fast-paced offense. A free-and-loose offense might have been the best for Davis because of his ridiculous athleticism and freakish length. However, Gentry was also known to rely more on the three-pointer. Because of that, questions were arising as to how he would utilize Davis's jumper. Would Davis start to venture out to the three-point area where he had only made 3 out of 27 shots over the past three seasons?

In addition to working on his three-point range during the offseason, Anthony also worked on his physique more. Davis modified his diet while focusing on weight training during the summer to add even more weight and strength to his frame. He hired a nutritionist who helped him improve his diet by adding more protein and calories to his daily intake. He also spent more time in the weight room while also working out with a strength and conditioning coach to make sure he retained the athletic frame that made him a freakish player.[vi]

With the offseason training he had, Davis packed on more pounds and weighed well over 250 pounds just three and a half years after scouts described him as a weak and skinny athlete. Now bigger and stronger than ever, AD was expected to better hold his own against opposing big men while also retaining the athleticism and explosiveness that had helped him become an elite star in the NBA.[vi] And adding to the reasons to fear him was the fact that he was also working on his three-point range in anticipation of the faster-paced style the team was moving toward. Yes, folks, it was time to fear the Brow!

Early in the season, it was becoming clear that Alvin Gentry had asked his superstar big man to shoot more from the outside to add more dimension and spacing to the offense. On October 28, 2015, his second game of the season, Davis scored 25 points and had 10 rebounds while making 3 of the 5 three-pointers he attempted. After making those three outside shots, he had already tied the totals he had from 2012 to 2015.

While Davis was venturing more outside the perimeter, he was still relying more on his efficient post-game and clean-looking mid-range jumper. In a loss to the Atlanta Hawks on November 5th, he went for 43 points, 10 rebounds, 3 assists, 4 steals, and 3 blocks for another ridiculous night. He was proving that he was worth every bit of that $145-million contract he had signed during the offseason.

After just winning one game in the Pelicans' first 12 outings, Davis went on to lead the team to what was a rare three-game winning streak for New Orleans that season. It started on November 20th when he had 20 points and a new season high of 18 rebounds versus the San Antonio Spurs. Davis immediately surpassed that output two nights later against the Phoenix Suns. He went for 32 points and 19 rebounds that night. And on November 25th, he went for 26 points and 17 rebounds versus the Suns once again.

During that stretch, he was averaging 26 points, 18 rebounds, and 2.7 blocks. Since winning that game against San Antonio, Davis was on his way to scoring in double digits for 22 consecutive games. The streak ended on January 8, 2016, in a loss to the Pacers.

As the season went on, Davis continued to play terrific basketball with his all-around offensive skillset. Not only was he posting up more often than he ever did but he was also attempting three-pointers at a rate that exceeded his past three seasons. Because of that, he was once again chosen as an All-Star player, although he was not a starter.

Davis took advantage of every second of the 15 minutes he played during the midseason classic. Davis thrived in that free-wheeling exhibition game by continually running to the basket for wide-open lob plays. He scored 24 points on 12 out of 13 shooting from the field to help lead the Western

Conference to a win. After the All-Star Break, Anthony Davis showed the complete package of his offense.

After scoring 34 points against the Philadelphia 76ers in a win on February 19th, Davis went into Detroit two days later with bad intentions. In what was a competitive game, the Pelicans regularly went to Davis for scoring opportunities. When they realized he was hot, the ball went through his hands on virtually every possession.

Davis took advantage of the Detroit Pistons' defense. Not even the large and athletic Andre Drummond could stop him. Davis took his defenders to school by draining shots over their heads out on the perimeter. When they tried to take his mid-range game, he beat his man to the basket with his dribble finishes or post-game. He even drained both of his three-pointers that night.

When the dust settled, New Orleans won that game against Detroit on the strength of perhaps the best performance Anthony Davis has ever had in his career. He made 24 of the 34 shots he attempted while also dominating on the rebounding end. He scored 59 points and grabbed 20 rebounds that night. His 59 points were the most that any player scored that season until Kobe Bryant had 60 points on the final day of the regular season.

After putting up 59 points and 20 rebounds that night, Davis also set a franchise record for points as well as the record for the youngest player in league history to score at least 59 in a game. He joined legends Shaquille O'Neal and Chris Webber as one of the only three players to have 50 points and 20 rebounds in a single game since 1983. Only he and Shaq scored at least 55 points and 20 rebounds in a game during that same period. That performance arguably made Anthony Davis the league's up-and-coming superstar big man.

But just when Davis was on a roll in that free-wheeling offense run by Alvin Gentry, he once again faced a setback. After playing 14 minutes in what would be a loss to the Portland Trail Blazers, he injured his knee. It was also then revealed that he had been suffering through a shoulder injury all season long. Because of that, the New Orleans Pelicans decided to shut their superstar down for the rest of the season.

After playing 61 games and missing the final 14 outings of the season, Anthony Davis averaged 24.3 points, 10.3 rebounds, 1.3 steals, and 2 blocks. While his field-goal shooting dropped to 49%, it was clear that he had become a better offensive player that season because he was taking and making more three-pointers under Gentry's pace-and-space style. He made 35 out of the 108 three-pointers he attempted after going for only 3 out of 27 in his previous three seasons. Davis also mixed things up with a combination of inside scoring and perimeter shooting.

While adjusting to Gentry's system, and with Davis missing games during the season, the New Orleans Pelicans dropped to 30 wins in that campaign. Sadly, they were far from playoff contention. And the fact of the matter was, even if they had Davis for the entire 82-game stretch, they were still missing the right pieces to make a push for a playoff spot. With role players such as Tyreke Evans, Jrue Holiday, and Ryan Anderson surrounding him, there was only so much that Davis could do for that team. What was evident was that the superstar big man needed capable help, no matter how elite he was on both ends of the floor.

Breaking the All-Star Game Record, the Trade for Boogie

The offseason was an unfruitful one for the New Orleans Pelicans in their quest to formulate a better-surrounding cast to work with Anthony Davis, the league's premier superstar big man. With only one playoff appearance under his belt, Davis may have been an elite player on both ends of the floor, but he was still far from the likes of LeBron James, Kevin Durant, Stephen Curry, and Russell Westbrook when it came to winning games. However, that did not stop Davis from imposing his will upon the NBA.

A healthy Anthony Davis, who had just recovered from his knee and shoulder injury, opened the season with one of the best performances in league history. Narrowly missing another five-by-five game, Davis put up 50 points, 15 rebounds, 5 assists, 5 steals, and 4 blocks in a loss to the Denver Nuggets on October 25th. He was the first player in league history to record at least 50 points, 15 rebounds, 5 assists, and 5 steals in a single game since 1973 when the league made steals and blocks official stats.

Davis did not rest after that historic opening game. Two days later, he tried to beat the Golden State Warriors on his own with 45 points, 17 rebounds, 2 steals, and 2 blocks. Nevertheless, that performance came at a loss. With that performance, he became the first player in league history to have back-to-back games of scoring at least 40 points.

Through the Pelicans' first eight games of the season, Davis averaged 30.9 points, 11.3 rebounds, 1.9 steals, and 2.9 blocks. No matter how great Davis was playing for the New Orleans Pelicans, the franchise could not get over the hump. They lost all of those first eight games, and it was becoming clear that Davis was a one-man show for the Pelicans.

Nevertheless, Davis went on to score 30 points and block 4 shots in Milwaukee on November 10th to give the Pelicans their first win of the season after that dismal 0-8 start. Though it was coming off a loss, Davis had 34 points two days later against the LA Lakers to complete a four-game stretch wherein he scored at least 30 points in consecutive games.

On November 23rd, Davis scored at least 40 points for the third time that season. Making 17 of his 27 shots in a win over the Minnesota Timberwolves, he went for 45 points to go along with 10 rebounds. Then, after scoring 31 and 36 points respectively in losses to the Trail Blazers and the Mavericks, Davis went for another 40-point game by scoring 41 points in a win over the Lakers. With that performance, Davis averaged 38.3 points and 13 rebounds in that four-game stretch.

After scoring and performing consistently on an individual level in the early part of the season, Davis went for his first 20-20 game of the season on December 23rd. In that win over the Miami Heat, he had 28 points and a career-high 22 rebounds. He then led the Pelicans to three more wins to secure a four-game winning streak wherein he averaged 28 points and 19 rebounds.

Davis started 2017 right by becoming a scoring and rebounding demon. In his first 4 games of the new year, he averaged 29 points and 17 rebounds. He punctuated that personal hot streak by going for 40 points, 18 rebounds, and 3 blocks in the Pelicans' win over the New York Knicks on January 9, 2017.

Davis had a momentous February that season as well. He started by going for 31 points and 12 rebounds in a loss to the Pistons on February 1st. Five days later, Davis had 34 points and 5 blocks in a win over the Phoenix Suns. And right before the All-Star Game, where he made his fourth appearance and

66

second as a starter, he had 42 points on February 10th in a win in Minnesota, and 32 points two days later in a loss to the Kings.

Davis's best performance was during the All-Star Game in front of the New Orleans fanbase. The hometown hero put on a show in front of the crowd before which he was so used to playing. Becoming an easy target for lob passes and in transition, he quietly dunked his way for a high-scoring performance. While plenty of attention went to Russell Westbrook, the season's leading MVP candidate, because he was seemingly on his way to becoming the first to break Wilt Chamberlain's record of 42 points in the midseason classic, Davis snuck by him.

Davis put on a show in the fourth quarter, as he was in his best state because of the lack of defense. Coming into the fourth quarter with 32 points while Westbrook was closer to Wilt's record, Davis dunked his way to 20 points in the final period to break a record that the Big Dipper had held since 1962. It took 55 years for someone to exceed those 42 points as Davis made 26 of his 39 shots to score a total of 52 points to lead the West to a win. Davis was the clear MVP of the All-Star Game after breaking a record that was almost untouchable for more than five decades. Jayson Tatum eventually broke this record in 2023. But it took several years before another All-Star during the modern era was able to touch Davis's record.

After the All-Star Game, it was then announced that New Orleans made a blockbuster trade to give Anthony Davis a fellow superstar that he could count on for production. As the Sacramento Kings realized that they were going nowhere with DeMarcus Cousins as their franchise player, they agreed to trade the superstar center to the Pelicans in exchange for rookie Buddy Hield, Tyreke Evans, and several draft picks. With Cousins now joining

Davis upfront, the Pelicans could not only give him a fellow superstar but also an imposing big man who made their frontline the best in the NBA.

Before the trade, Anthony Davis was averaging 27.7 points, while Cousins was averaging 27.8 points. The two big men were in the top five in scoring and were merely behind Russell Westbrook, James Harden, and Isaiah Thomas in that regard. Individually, both of those players were already unstoppable in their own rights. After all, Davis was the best power forward, while Cousins was the best center in the NBA at that time. Teaming up in the frontcourt only meant that no other big-man tandem in the league could contend with them.

Because the NBA was getting smaller and smaller to adjust to the faster pace and the emphasis on three-point shooting, big men have found themselves playing lesser roles. There were only a few elite power forwards and centers left in the NBA since most big men were designated floor stretchers, rebounders, and defenders only. However, as the two best big men in the league were set to team up in New Orleans, it was becoming clear that the rest of the NBA's frontline defense had to step up to contend with the dominance of the Pelicans' superstar, super-sized duo.

With DeMarcus Cousins in the fold, there was a reason to believe that the New Orleans Pelicans were ready to make a push for one of the final playoff spots in the West. However, they still needed to adjust. The two Kentucky products upfront needed to get to know each other's tendencies first before they could lead the Pelicans to a playoff appearance.

Of course, even though the Pelicans now had Cousins, the league's most imposing center, Davis was still the man. In his first game with Cousins, Davis had 39 points and 14 rebounds in a loss to the Dallas Mavericks on

February 25th. A night later, he went for 38 points in a losing effort versus the OKC Thunder.

While DeMarcus Cousins was a great scorer in his own right, what those first two games showed was that he was content to be a passer as well. As one of the most gifted passing big men in the league, he was finding open opportunities for Davis, who was more available than usual because of how Cousins was also attracting defensive attention and because of his sheer dominance and ability to hit the open jump shot.

On March 11th, Anthony Davis had a dominant performance while Cousins was still finding his way. Davis made 18 of his 31 shots and 4 of his 5 three-pointers in that win over the Charlotte Hornets to score 46 points. He also added 21 rebounds to his name to record the second time in his career that he had at least 40 points and 20 rebounds.

Because the New Orleans Pelicans were still a few miles away from becoming playoff contenders, the team sat Anthony Davis out in the final three games of the season, marking the fourth time in his career wherein he missed the final few games of the regular season. (But at least this time it was not because of injuries!) The Pelicans were winners of only 34 games that season despite adding Cousins to the lineup.

At the end of his fifth season, the 23-year-old big man averaged career highs in points and rebounds after averaging 28 points and 11.8 boards. He also added 2.1 assists, 1.3 steals, and 2.2 blocks to his name. While Davis was putting up better numbers than he ever did, what was most impressive was that he played more than 70 games for the first time in his career. Davis appeared in 75 games that season and missed just seven outings. Before that season, the most games he played in a season was only 68. Playing 75 games meant that Davis might have already moved past his injury woes and health issues.

Despite not making the playoffs for the fourth time in his five-year career, Anthony Davis was named to the All-NBA first team for the second time in his career. He was also named to the All-Defensive second team as a testament to how well he played defense by blocking shots and stealing possessions with his long arms and terrific timing. With Cousins joining on a full-time basis next season, there was a reason to believe Davis had more room and energy to operate on both ends of the floor. Things were looking up for the Pelicans.

Teaming Up with Cousins on the NBA's Best Frontline, Breaking Past the First Round

After another season of missing the playoffs, there were not many positives that Anthony Davis could take out of that 2016-17 season. However, a superstar teammate in DeMarcus "Boogie" Cousins should have made him hopeful. Like Davis, Cousins had developed himself to become one of the most dominant players in the NBA, but he never did see much luck as far as team success was concerned. Now, the two best big men in the entire NBA had the chance to rule the league's paint while hoping to lead the New Orleans Pelicans to a playoff berth.

However, some said that the Davis-Cousins tandem was going to be an experiment. DeMarcus Cousins was heading into the 2017-18 season on the final year of his contract. Considering that he had been the NBA's best center, several teams undoubtedly lined up to court him during the free agency period. To avoid losing Cousins, the Pelicans needed the dominant tandem to work well together.

As Alvin Gentry said, both Davis and Cousins wanted the tandem to work. Cousins may have had some history with his temper, but he was always an unselfish player. The same could be said about Anthony Davis, who was never shy about deferring to his teammates during specific periods of the game. Both Davis and Boogie were always willing passers for their size. If they understood each other's tendencies, the expectation was for the two Kentucky products to find each other whenever defenses swarmed either one of them.

With the NBA trending toward small ball for more speed and spacing, the tandem of Davis and Cousins was a fresh sight for fans who missed the old days when the best teams had two dominant big men up front. Ordinarily, a twin-tower lineup would be at a disadvantage in today's NBA because of how much faster teams play and how much emphasis had been placed on three-point shooting. However, the Davis-Cousins frontline was different.

Unlike the twin-tower duos of Sampson-Olajuwon, Robinson-Duncan, and Gasol-Bynum, the AD and Boogie tandem was much different. They may be as big and tall as traditional big men, but their style was anything but old school. While both Davis and Cousins could play inside the paint for post opportunities, they relied heavily on their versatility.

Both players are unicorns—big and tall forwards or centers that have the skills of a guard. Anthony Davis's ability to shoot the mid-range jumper and drive to the basket from the perimeter has been well-documented ever since he broke out during the 2013-14 season. He improved his game down at the low post while also venturing out on the three-pointer more often than he ever did. Because he is so athletic and long, Davis was always practically unstoppable when he got deep position.

Meanwhile, DeMarcus Cousins's game was not much different. Using his size, strength, and heft, Cousins came into the NBA relying on his post scoring. However, he had also learned how to shoot the three-pointer well. For a 6'10" center, he shot 36% from the three-point line during the 2016-17 season. Because Cousins could also put the ball on the floor, opposing big men were always wary about closing out on him. Moreover, Boogie always had an uncanny passing ability for a man of his size.

Clogging the paint was also never going to be a problem for the Pelicans. The problem with teams that played two post players was spacing. With two big men waiting near the basket for drop passes and lobs, there was not much room for guards to operate and space for the pair of seven-footers to move around the basket. Since both Davis and Cousins could take their game out on the perimeter, spacing was not a problem. Either one of them could act as a floor-spacer while the other waited near the basket for lobs and drop passes. It was a marriage that was bound to be successful.

Because both Anthony Davis and DeMarcus Cousins were always so versatile concerning skills and athleticism, the New Orleans Pelicans adjusted well to how the NBA has been playing small ball while retaining the size to dominate opposing frontlines. Davis's athleticism allowed him to close out to the likes of Draymond Green and Kevin Love out on the perimeter while using his length to disrupt passes and block shots. Meanwhile, Cousins mobility allowed him to keep up with centers that ventured out from the paint. In short, the Pelicans had size without losing versatility.

When the season began, the two big men immediately showed why they were the cream of the crop at their respective positions. On opening day, which was a loss to the Memphis Grizzlies on October 18, 2017, both Davis and Boogie played well. Davis finished with 33 points and 18 rebounds. Meanwhile, Cousins had 28 points, 10 rebounds, and 7 blocks.

The tandem got their first win of the season on October 22nd against the Lakers. Anthony had a beautiful stat line after going for 27 points, 17 rebounds, 3 assists, 3 steals, and 3 blocks. Meanwhile, Cousins found his identity as the team's playmaking big man after going for 22 points, 11 rebounds, and 8 assists. Boogie had an easy time finding open looks for Davis because of how defenses were shying away from double-teaming either one of them.

On October 28th, the pair had another fantastic outing as a duo when they dominated the much smaller Cleveland Cavaliers frontline. Anthony Davis had 30 points, 14 rebounds, and 3 blocks in that blowout win. Meanwhile, DeMarcus Cousins finished with a triple-double after going for 29 points, 12 rebounds, and 10 assists. The two big men were more than comfortable playing off and with each other because of their diverse skills.

With DeMarcus Cousins in the fold attracting defenses while finding open looks for Davis, Anthony Davis became an even more efficient scorer. He was scoring big on fewer attempts. A good example was when Davis had 37 points on 14 out of 18 shooting from the field in the Pelicans' win against the Indiana Pacers on November 7th. At that point, he was shooting nearly 57% from the floor in his first 10 games while averaging over 28 points a night.

Davis continued to play efficient basketball because of how well Cousins was also playing off of him. Though Boogie was a significant factor as far as rebounding, scoring, and playmaking were concerned, the primary scoring punch was still Davis. More importantly, the big-men tandem was also leading the Pelicans to a winning record.

On January 12, 2018, Davis began a dominant three-game stretch for himself while also leading his team to three consecutive wins. In a win over the Portland Trail Blazers, he went for 36 points and 9 rebounds. Two nights later, Davis helped beat the New York Knicks in overtime by finishing with a new season-high 48 points along with 14 rebounds, 4 steals, and 3 blocks. On January 15, 2019, he went for 45 points and 16 rebounds in a win over the East-leading Boston Celtics.

Because of how dominant both Anthony Davis and DeMarcus Cousins were throughout the entire season, they were both voted in as starters for the 2018 All-Star Game. With the new format in play, they were also both drafted by LeBron James to play for his team in the midseason classic. Fans were hoping to see the same chemistry and jaw-dropping plays they had been displaying in New Orleans in the All-Star Game in Los Angeles.

However, misfortune was quick to strike just when the Pelicans were surging. In a win over a hot Houston Rockets team on January 25th, Cousins chased down a loose ball and got injured in the process. Boogie was carried off the court and was unable to return to the game.

It was soon revealed that Boogie had ruptured his Achilles tendon and would miss the remainder of the season. Just when things had looked bright for the Pelicans, one of their superstars suffered a setback that could potentially derail the entire team and jeopardize their season.

So, with Cousins out, AD was once again left as the team's lone superstar. The Pelicans, by this point, actually had a good chance to make the playoffs thanks to how well Cousins had been playing with Davis—but now they were placed in a bleak position because of their new star's injury. Nevertheless, Davis was already long used to leading New Orleans alone.

Averaging 26.8 points on 54% shooting while also norming 10.6 rebounds, 2.5 assists, 1.2 steals, and 2.1 blocks, Davis was in the middle of one of his best and most productive seasons as he neared his prime as a basketball player. If there was ever a perfect time for AD to prove his worth as a leader and prove that he was an elite superstar in the league, it was then and there when the team lost Cousins. A run for a playoff spot and a strong showing in the playoffs without Boogie would undoubtedly solidify his claim as one of the best and brightest stars in the entire league.

Davis started his quest to solidify his status in the NBA by etching his name into New Orleans franchise history books with a record-setting feat. On January 28th, in a loss to the Los Angeles Clippers, he grabbed a total of 17 rebounds and ended the night as the Pelicans' all-time leading rebounder. He eclipsed David West's record in that game, and it would not be the only time he broke records that season!

Without Cousins, Anthony Davis moved up to play the center position and could play it well, just like he always had. On February 2nd, he had 43 points and 10 rebounds in a win over the Oklahoma City Thunder. That performance made Davis the franchise's all-time leading scorer as well. He followed that up with 38 points in a losing effort over the Minnesota Timberwolves just a day after that phenomenal performance.

On February 10th, Davis started an incredible run that saw him posting ridiculous numbers for the Pelicans. In a win over the Brooklyn Nets, he finished with a crazy stat line of 44 points, 17 rebounds, 6 steals, and 3 blocks. Then, in the next two games, he finished with 38 and 42 points respectively before leading a win over the Miami Heat on February 23rd with 45 points, 17 rebounds, 5 steals, and 5 blocks.

After a 27-point performance in a win over the Milwaukee Bucks on February 25th, Davis went for another ridiculous game. In that win over the Phoenix Suns, he had 53 points, 18 rebounds, 3 assists, and 5 blocks. That performance capped off a tremendous six-game stretch that saw him averaging 41.5 points, 15 rebounds, 3 steals, and 3.2 blocks. More importantly, he led his team to a 10-game winning streak, showing that he did not necessarily need Boogie by his side to get the job done.

Anthony Davis scored 30 or more points in the final 21 games of the 2017-18 regular season. During those final stretches, he scored 41 points in a win over the Los Angeles Clippers. Those 21 games also saw Davis posting his first career triple-double when he had 25 points, 11 rebounds, and 10 blocks in a loss to the Utah Jazz on March 11th. He had a total of six blocks in just one half of that game.

Because of his great performances to end the season, especially after the New Orleans Pelicans lost DeMarcus Cousins to injury just before the All-Star Break, Anthony Davis could improve his numbers. As the team's de facto center, he averaged 28.1 points, 11.1 rebounds, 2.3 assists, 1.5 steals, and 2.6 blocks while shooting 53.4% from the floor. Since Cousins' injury, Davis averaged 30.2 points and 12 rebounds.

That season, Davis was only second to James Harden in points per game. He also finished second to Harden in terms of player efficiency rating. As such, there was no denying the fact that Anthony Davis was one of the greatest individual players in the NBA that season. More importantly, the New Orleans Pelicans made a return trip to the playoffs under his phenomenal leadership and play all season long.

In the first round of the playoffs against the Portland Trail Blazers, Anthony Davis and the New Orleans Pelicans were on full throttle, as they did not fold to the team with the higher seed and home-court advantage. Hunger drove Davis to perform at his very best against the Blazers as he used his rare and unique abilities to force mismatches against Portland's big men.

Davis finished Game 1 in Portland with 35 points, 14 rebounds, 2 steals, and 4 blocks as the Pelicans ended up drawing first blood. While many thought the third-seeded Blazers eventually struck back against the sixth-seeded Pelicans, Davis did it on both ends of the floor once again. In Game 2, he had 22 points, 12 rebounds, 2 steals, and 2 blocks to finish the first two games in Portland with wins.

Back home in New Orleans, Davis played to the tempo of the crowd's roar, as he was hungry to taste playoff success for the first time in his entire NBA career. He had 28 points, 11 rebounds, 3 steals, and 2 blocks in that Game 3 win, earning a surefire trip to the second round with that 3-0 lead over the Blazers. Davis did not waste any time kicking the Portland Trail Blazers out of the playoffs after he finished Game 4 with a playoff career high and a franchise playoff record of 47 points in addition to 10 rebounds and 3 blocks.

Averaging 33 points, 11.8 rebounds, 1.8 steals, and 2.8 blocks in that first-round encounter against the Blazers, Anthony Davis proved to be the difference-maker on both ends.

While Jrue Holiday and his other teammates made it difficult for Damian Lillard to operate out on the perimeter, AD was the real deterrent that prevented anyone from attacking the basket. Moreover, he used his ability to create mismatches to full advantage, and Portland's centers were far too slow-footed to keep up with him. When matched with power forwards, Davis overpowered them or used his superior size and length to his advantage.

Those were the same attributes he would need to take advantage of in the second-round encounter against the formidable Golden State Warriors, who were the winners of two of the last three championships at that point—and the Dubs appeared to be on a tear once again.

While Anthony Davis still did a terrific job as the primary source of offense and defense for the New Orleans Pelicans in their series against the Warriors, their four All-Stars were still too much for a team with only one superstar. The Pelicans won just one game, which was Game 3 in New Orleans. Davis finished that game with 33 points, 18 rebounds, and 4 steals.

The Golden State Warriors ended up beating the Pelicans in only five games. In Game 5, Davis tried to singlehandedly bring the team back from their losses, but there was only so much that a lone star could do. (Could a healthy Cousins working alongside Davis in those games have made a difference? It is possible, but sadly, we'll never know.)

Davis finished Game 5 with 34 points, 19 rebounds, and 3 blocks as the Warriors defeated them and eventually won the NBA title that season. In that five-game series, Davis averaged 27.8 points, 14.8 rebounds, 2.2 steals, and 2 blocks. Davis had clearly given it his all and had carried the Pelicans on his own much farther than anyone had truly expected—but it was also clear that he needed help.

Though the season was already over for AD after losing to the Warriors, the awards were still to be decided. With the terrific performances he put up all season long while leading the New Orleans Pelicans back to the playoffs even after losing DeMarcus Cousins, Anthony Davis was worthy of getting named as a finalist for not just one award but two—the Most Valuable Player and the Defensive Player of the Year Awards.

Along with James Harden and LeBron James, Davis was a finalist for the MVP. Yet, he did not only do things on the offensive end. Davis was also a beast on the defensive end of the floor as he was nominated as a finalist for the DPOY Award as well, alongside centers Rudy Gobert of the Utah Jazz and Joel Embiid of the Philadelphia 76ers.

James Harden had a strong case to be named MVP too that season. He led the NBA's best regular-season team while leading the league in points per game and player efficiency rating. On the other hand, LeBron James, who was getting older at that time, also was a solid choice for MVP as he was defying time and putting up great performances and ridiculous stats for the Cleveland Cavaliers.

However, Anthony Davis himself could make a pretty good case as the MVP that season. Whether he was playing alongside DeMarcus Cousins or was the lone star playing the center position for the New Orleans Pelicans, Davis was affecting the floor at an elite level. He was putting points up on the board with such regularity using his combination of size, strength, length, mobility, athleticism, and skill. Davis was a matchup nightmare for any big man in the league, regardless of whether he was playing power forward or center. Finishing second in points per game and player efficiency rating proved that Davis was as elite as anyone in the NBA could get.

What really set Anthony Davis apart from the other two contenders for the MVP award was his ability to affect the game at both ends of the floor. Among the top three finalists for the MVP, Davis was the only one who finished in the top 10 in offensive win shares and defensive win shares. He was the only player in the league to do such that season, as many players would instead focus on either the offensive end or the defensive end. While that does not mean that James Harden and LeBron James are bad defenders, it does point out that Anthony Davis was efficient both on offense and defense. You can also add the fact that he almost singlehandedly brought the Pelicans back to the playoffs.

As for the Defensive Player of the Year Award, Anthony Davis also put up an active campaign all season long. When it comes to defending the basket, no other player in the league came close to Rudy Gobert. Meanwhile, Joel Embiid was also no slouch on the defensive end that season, as his mere hulking presence was enough to deter anyone from attacking the basket. However, they did not have the same all-around defensive season that Davis had.

In an era where teams have become switch-heavy on the defensive end to try to prevent guards from getting the opening they need to get a shot off after a pick-and-roll play, Anthony Davis is the ideal big man. On top of how well he uses his long arms and great timing to swat away shots at a league-leading level, Davis was always an adept perimeter defender because of his mobility and his length. That said, he can guard all positions on the floor well and is only one of a handful of players who could do so at an elite level.

However, because NBA awards are also determined by how well a player could contribute to his team's success, Anthony Davis ended up finishing third in both awards because all the players he was up against had better team records. Davis ultimately lost the MVP Award to James Harden that year, while Rudy Gobert ended up getting named the DPOY. Nevertheless, Anthony Davis's standout play all season long as well as his phenomenal efforts in the postseason will undoubtedly be a highlight of his career that fans will not soon forget.

Despite failing to secure a major individual award that season, Anthony Davis was named to the All-NBA first team for the third time as well as to the All-Defensive first team for the first time in his career. Of course, getting named as a finalist for both of those awards only proved that Davis was one of the greatest two-way players in the league at that time and, alongside names such as Kawhi Leonard and Paul George, was the best all-around offensive and defensive threat in the entire NBA.

The biggest question at this point in his career was whether or not Davis could keep playing at an elite level on both ends of the floor without succumbing to the frustrations of leading a team that was practically going nowhere as far as wins were concerned. The Pelicans may have broken into the second round during the 2018 playoffs, but frankly, nobody expected them to do so in the next few seasons consistently. Because New Orleans is the smallest market in the NBA, nobody believed that a star as big as Davis could keep shining bright in such a small market without getting compensated with wins.

That said, it seemed as if Davis's days with the New Orleans Pelicans were numbered, especially in an era where superstars put more emphasis on joining a winning culture and teaming up with fellow stars who could help them solidify their legacies as champions. Simply put, the Pelicans had a chance to do that when they acquired DeMarcus Cousins—their *final* chance.

The Final Season in New Orleans

During the offseason of 2018, the New Orleans Pelicans did not bring DeMarcus Cousins back. The center, who was recovering from his injury, signed a discounted deal with the Golden State Warriors instead. What that ultimately meant was that the Pelicans were officially down to one star once again. And if history were any indication, they were not going to go far by relying merely on Anthony Davis.

Being the superstar that he is, Anthony Davis put the team on his back even though he once again did not have enough help that season. He once again played center as he was sharing the frontcourt with the young and improving big man Julius Randle, whom the Pelicans acquired during the offseason when the Lakers decided not to renew his contract after securing LeBron James' services.

Davis made his 2018-19 season debut on October 17, 2019, against the Houston Rockets. In that win over last year's best regular-season team, Davis finished with 32 points, 16 rebounds, 8 assists, 3 steals, and 3 blocks to record another ridiculous stat line that only he could achieve in the NBA at that time. He then helped the Pelicans win the next three games to race ahead to a 4-0 start to the season. In those four games, Davis averaged 27.3 points, 13.3 rebounds, 4.8 assists, 2.5 steals, and 3.8 blocks.

However, after a quick 4-0 start, the New Orleans Pelicans began to slow down, and they ended up losing the next six games. Davis missed half of those six games due to injury but was not hampered enough to fail to perform at the top of his abilities during the early part of the season.

On November 12th, Davis had his first 20-20 game that season. He finished that win over the Toronto Raptors with 25 points, 20 rebounds, and 6 assists. Then, four days later, Davis finished a win over the New York Knicks with a new season-high 43 points to go along with 17 rebounds and 5 assists. A night later, he followed that up with 40 points, 8 rebounds, and 8 assists after hitting 20 of his 21 free throws in a win over the Denver Nuggets.

Anthony Davis did not need to wait long to put up 40 or more points once again. On November 30th, he finished a loss to the Miami Heat with 40 points. Then, in the next game, he narrowly missed a triple-double after going for 36 points, 19 rebounds, 8 assists, 2 steals, and 2 blocks in a win over the Charlotte Hornets. In his first 20 games of the season, Davis averaged 28.2 points, 13 rebounds, 4.8 assists, 1.6 steals, and 2.7 blocks.

While Davis's early-season stats indicated that he was still playing at an elite level on both ends, it also demonstrated that he had grown in a field in which he had never truly excelled in the past—*passing*. That season, Davis showed plenty of commitment as a playmaker as there were moments when he sought out his teammates first, before looking for his own shots. As such, he had 6 or more assists in 9 of his first 20 games that season. In three of those games, he had eight assists after failing to register one game of at least eight assists last season.

Averaging two assists a game his entire career before the 2018-19 season, it was clear that AD did not put much emphasis on his playmaking abilities. After all, he spent the majority of his first few seasons as a receiver and finisher instead of a player who could make plays with the ball in his hands. In the last two seasons, however, Davis began showing what he could do as a superstar who could create scoring opportunities for himself when he has enough room to operate whenever he has the ball in his hands.

The eye test would tell you that Davis was never a lousy passer or a black hole on offense. After all, he was brought up as a point guard during his younger years before he suddenly grew taller. So, in addition to his mobility and ball-handling skills, Davis has the fundamental skills of a solid playmaker. However, because his focus the last few seasons was to finish baskets whenever he had the ball in his hands, he did not have many opportunities to make plays for others.

However, during the 2018-19 season, it was clear that Davis was already trying to make an effort as a playmaker. Operating from the post, he could easily see what was happening on the floor from his point of view and could make passes to open teammates. Whenever teams tried to take him out of his game by doubling him, there was no reason for him to force the issue all by himself.

For Davis that season, it was all about trusting that his teammates could finish baskets whenever defenses converged on him. He may never end up being the playmaker that LeBron James is or the post passer that Nikola Jokic is, but the most significant improvement in Davis's game that season was that he was always making the right reads and making the right passes. After all, that is what superstars should do. The best stars never force their way out of a tough situation and always take what is available, which includes making plays for teammates.

Pelicans head coach Alvin Gentry said that Davis was learning not to play against multiple defenders and was compensating by making the right plays for his teammates.[vii] He did not only pass the ball when he had no other choice. Davis was reading defenses more so than he ever did and was making plays for his teammates the moment other defenders began reacting to his movements.

For example, he surveys the floor thoroughly before even taking his first dribble when he has the ball at the low post. The moment Davis sees a help defender reacting when he is driving to the basket, Davis already knows to whom he should pass the ball. There were even moments where he was the pick-and-roll ball-handler instead of playing the role of the roll guy. Simply put, AD showed that his game was still growing and that he was developing as a playmaker as well.

Despite improving as a passer, Anthony Davis was and *is* still a scorer. On December 10th, he finished a loss to the Boston Celtics with 41 points. Two nights later, Davis led a win over the Oklahoma City Thunder with 44 points, 18 rebounds, and 2 steals. Then, on December 28th in a win over the Dallas Mavericks, he recorded a new season high of 48 points along with 17 rebounds, 4 assists, 2 steals, and 2 blocks. That game saw him hitting the winning fading jumper with less than 44 seconds left on the clock.

After that December 28th performance, Davis continued to wreak havoc. He scored 30 or more points in all but three of his next nine outings. In one of those nine games, he finished with 46 points and 16 rebounds in a win over the Los Angeles Clippers. Also, in the middle of that run, Davis had a career high and a franchise high of 26 rebounds in a loss to the Brooklyn Nets on January 2, 2019.

Davis averaged 29.3 points, 13.3 rebounds, 4.4 assists, 1.7 steals, and 2.6 blocks at that point of the season. He was well on his way to shattering his previous highs in points, rebounds, and assists in a single season.

Davis then missed nine consecutive games with an injured index finger. It was also during that time when he told the New Orleans Pelicans that he had no plans of re-signing with the team during the upcoming offseason, and thus would become an unrestricted free agent in the offseason of 2020. In effect,

Anthony Davis had requested a trade from the New Orleans Pelicans front office.[viii]

While Davis recovered from his finger injury after he made his trade request public, the New Orleans Pelicans kept him inactive until they could find a suitable trade partner before the expiry of the trade deadline on February 7, 2019.

The Los Angeles Lakers franchise was Anthony Davis's preferred destination. Luckily, the Lakers had enough assets to try to make a move to acquire Davis, and to team him up with the legendary LeBron James.

While people were thinking that Davis was inevitably going to end up wearing a purple and gold uniform after the trade deadline, the talks between the Pelicans and the Lakers ended prematurely when the latter front office thought that New Orleans was asking too much for the superstar power forward/center. So, in effect, no trade between the Pelicans and the Lakers ever materialized that season. Furthermore, no other team had enough assets to try to convince the Pelicans to part with the league's best big man.

On February 8th, Anthony Davis made his return to the lineup after the injury and the trade request. He finished that win over the Minnesota Timberwolves with 32 points and 9 rebounds. However, that seemed to be the only significant performance he had after asking to be traded, considering that his future with the team was already bleak and that he was also suffering through multiple minor injuries.

Finally, in the middle of March, the team decided to shut Davis down in the hopes of preserving his health in the long run, as the New Orleans Pelicans were not going to reach the playoffs that season. Since returning after his trade request, Davis played in only 15 games and averaged 16.6 points and 8.5 rebounds while playing only a little over 22 minutes a night.

After his hot start that season, Davis ultimately regressed in terms of the numbers he was putting up. Of course, this was mainly because of lingering injuries, but it was also partly because of the hopeless future he had with the Pelicans and all the disappointment that entailed. He was simply a trade asset waiting to be materialized, and the team knew that they needed him to be at 100% if they wanted to get the most out of his value during the offseason.

Davis averaged 25.9 points along with career highs of 12 rebounds and 3.9 assists that season. While not substandard, his numbers could have been better had it not been for the injuries and the inevitable looming trade. He played his final game for the Pelicans on March 24th and finished that night with 12 rebounds and 10 assists in a loss to the Houston Rockets.

The Trade to the Lakers, the Championship Run in the Bubble

During the offseason of 2019, the New Orleans Pelicans won the draft lottery and managed to get the No. 1 overall pick, Duke freshman standout Zion Williamson. Teaming Williamson with Anthony Davis at the frontcourt would have given New Orleans the league's most physically talented tandem in the league. However, that duo did not materialize.

Even before the day of the draft came, the New Orleans Pelicans decided to part ways with Anthony Davis after they indeed confirmed that the superstar big man had no plans of extending his stay with the team beyond 2020. As such, they traded him to the Los Angeles Lakers for a very lucrative package that included Lonzo Ball, Brandon Ingram (the second-overall draft pick of 2016), and three future first-round draft picks.

For Anthony Davis's part, he left New Orleans as arguably the greatest superstar the franchise has ever seen. But, the same as any other star the beleaguered franchise has seen, AD was not able to lead them to a deep playoff run. Nevertheless, the onus of the team's ongoing failures was not Anthony's burden to carry. He had done all he could for them, and he ended his tenure as a Pelican leading the franchise in almost all statistical categories except in assists and steals. The simple truth was, a superstar of his caliber deserved to be in a winning culture and with a franchise that could give him the championships that would cement his career. The Pelicans were just not there yet.

"Money comes and goes; your legacy is forever," was what Anthony Davis said upon his move to Los Angeles.

He could have potentially made more money if he had stayed in New Orleans, but at the end of the day, what Davis valued more than money was his legacy as a superstar. Davis knew that what people would remember about the greatest basketball players in history is not the money they made over their careers but rather the accomplishments that they achieved.[ix] Ask anyone about Michael Jordan and there is a 99% chance that they do not know how much money he earned in his NBA career, but there is much certainty that they will know the number of championships His Airness has won. That was the type of respect that Anthony Davis was trying to earn by asking to be traded to the Lakers.

Moving to the Los Angeles Lakers meant that Anthony Davis was going to play alongside LeBron James, who was still regarded as the best player in the league at that time, despite missing the 2019 Playoffs. It also meant that, for the first time in his NBA career, Davis was going to have to share the floor with a more accomplished player.

There was no question that the tandem of Anthony Davis and LeBron James was going to work. Individually, both players were arguably the best at their respective positions. Save for names such as Kevin Durant and Kawhi Leonard, you will not be able to find any small forward at the level of James's greatness in the NBA. He has a complete offensive game, a well-conditioned body, and the passing skills of a superstar point guard.

Meanwhile, there is not much left to say about Anthony Davis that has not already been said. AD is a force at both ends of the floor and can play both big men positions at a high level. On offense, he is as great a player with the ball as he is without it. That is because he knows how to opportunistically cut to the basket, run to the rim when the ball-handler absorbs the defense, and score off offensive rebounds as well.

On top of that, Davis is reliable with the ball in his hands both on the low and high posts, where he can either drive to the basket, hit a post shot, or look for open teammates as an improved playmaker. And the best part of it all? Davis, at just 26 years old, was still at the prime of his career when he was traded to the Lakers.

That said, Davis was going to be an excellent running mate for LeBron James, who had not had a megastar teammate since Dwyane Wade. However, what was going to be special about this tandem was that Davis did not demand the ball as much as Dwyane Wade or Kyrie Irving. His ability to hit open jumpers and cut to the basket strong to finish on dunks and layups are assets that any great passer such as James would love to have in his teammates.

In fact, since 2015, Davis has scored 3,316 points on assisted two-pointers. No other player in the league has even touched the 3,000 mark in that stat, even though Davis missed several games since 2015. Moreover, during the 2017-18 season, only Kristaps Porzingis and Karl-Anthony Towns were able to score 20 or more points with fewer seconds and dribbles per touch than Anthony Davis.[x]

What does all that mean? It merely means that Davis is a phenomenal offensive player, regardless of whether or not he has the ball in his hands. He did not need the ball to be effective because he could play both off and on the ball without problems. On the ball, he was a problem because he could match up with power forwards and centers alike and become a mismatch for them with his speed, strength, and athleticism. Off the ball, he excels at cutting to the basket or playing the pick-and-roll. Moreover, with LeBron James attracting plenty of defensive attention, finding his spots on the floor was not going to be difficult for Davis.

What also made Anthony Davis the perfect teammate for James was his ability to defend all spots on the floor at a high level. James has never had a teammate who could not only score at an elite level but could also impact the defensive end of the floor better than almost any other big man in the league. Dwyane Wade himself was a phenomenal offensive player and a great defender. But not even Wade had the same kind of defensive impact that Davis had. That said, Davis was going to make up for the defensive lapses that were evident from James in his declining years.

Speaking of LeBron James' age, perhaps Davis's greatest asset at that time was his youth. Joining the Lakers at 26 years old, he was at the prime of his career and was still improving. Meanwhile, the 34-year-old LeBron, despite being one of the greatest players in league history, was not going to get any younger, faster, or more athletic. So, in a sense, having Davis in the fold was a security blanket for the Los Angeles Lakers, as they were hoping for a megastar to emerge that could take over James' role once his advancing age finally caught up with him. In short, Anthony Davis was going to be one of the faces that would carry the Lakers into the future.

Of course, that 2019-20 Lakers team had the makings of a championship squad. With Frank Vogel at the helm of the coaching staff, that was supposed to be a tough defensive team because Vogel was known for his defensive squads when he was with the Indiana Pacers. The Lakers also added several veterans that were hungry for titles. These names included Danny Green, Dwight Howard, and JaVale McGee. And because the team had legit centers, Davis was now going to return to his natural position of power forward.

Having Davis playing power forward together with either Howard or McGee allowed Vogel to have a strong frontcourt that could defend the paint and own rebounds. While Howard and McGee were not entirely great offensive threats, they were lob threats for LeBron. And the best part was that they alleviated defensive pressure on Davis because they were going to be the ones who were tasked to defend opposing centers and bang bodies with other big men inside the paint.

In that regard, Davis's role as a defender was on the *help* side because he did not have to bang bodies with other centers to play defense. Instead, what he now had to do was patrol nearby and help his teammates whenever they needed someone to quickly cover the paint and block or bother shots. He was also quick enough to recover to perimeter players in case the ball found itself outside. And because AD was always known to be somewhat injury-prone, alleviating that pressure also decreased the load and stress on his body.

Another big change that Vogel instituted into that Lakers team was putting LeBron James at the point guard spot so that the wings would be filled up by shooters. LeBron was always known as a ball-dominant player. even at the small forward position, because he could pass better than most guards and was great at creating plays for himself and others. So, with LeBron manning the point, he now had complete control over the ball and was going to be the person in charge of setting Davis up for easy baskets. Thus, basketball had never been so easy for Davis! He now had a true all-time great as a teammate who could attract defensive attention and make plays for him from the point.

In his first season with the Lakers, Davis focused more on picking his spots and playing help defense because he no longer had to be the focal point of the offense. As such, the offense seemed so natural to him because he only had to play off LeBron and his other teammates. On October 29, 2019, AD went for a massive performance of 40 points and 20 rebounds in a win over the Memphis Grizzlies. He hit 26 of the 27 foul shots that he attempted in that game and was a clear matchup nightmare for the entire Grizzlies team.

On November 27th, Davis went for another massive scoring performance by going for 41 points in his return trip to New Orleans in what was his first game against the Pelicans since the trade. Davis dominated his former team in what seemed to be a performance with personal feelings involved. And with his help, the Lakers went on to win 18 of their first 20 games and, it was clear that LA were now favorites to win the championship that season.

In another great game for Davis, he went for 39 points against the Portland Trail Blazers on December 6th. Just after that performance, he dominated the Minnesota Timberwolves by going for a new season high of 50 points in a win. Then, on January 3, 2020, he went for 46 points and 13 rebounds in another dominant performance against his old team.

On January 26, 2020, arguably the greatest Laker of all time perished in a helicopter crash. Kobe Bryant was confirmed to have been killed together with his second daughter, Gigi, while he and several other passengers were on their way to a basketball clinic. His death had a huge effect on the entire NBA and several players went on to dedicate games and performances to his memory. But the Lakers turned the entire season into a mission to honor one of the greatest winners in the sport of basketball. Nothing short of a championship that season would allow the Lakers to pay their respects to Kobe Bryant's memory. To them, Bryant was much more than a basketball hero—he was *family*. The iconic Bryant had spent his entire 20-year career as a Laker.

However, the LA Lakers needed to wait a bit longer to win a championship in honor of their fallen Laker great. That was because the COVID-19 pandemic was sweeping the world at this time and was taking its toll on many organized sports. The NBA was forced to suspend the 2019-20 season on March 11, 2020, after Rudy Gobert became the first person to contract the potentially lethal virus. As such, the league had to suspend its operations and mandate all players to stay in quarantine until more information was released regarding the virus and what the NBA would do in relation to the continuation of the season.

During the quarantine period, Davis took some time off to relax because he was always prone to injury. That season alone, he had missed eight games due to minor injuries. Knowing that he was the most important piece of the Lakers' championship hopes due to his presence on both ends of the floor, the one thing that he needed to focus on the most was his health. The time off from the game allowed him to rest his body, especially because he was already at the prime of his prowess at the age of 27.

He even joked about how he only spent the entire quarantine period eating burgers and relaxing. While some of the other stars in the NBA tried to stay in good shape while waiting for the season to resume, Davis simply rested because his availability was always his best ability. The Lakers would rather allow Davis to rest and relax so that he could be at 100% instead of not having him at all.

In June, the different stakeholders of the NBA were able to come to an agreement on what they needed to do to address the COVID-19 situation. The goal was to continue the season in a "Bubble" in Orlando, Florida. Only the top eight teams of each Conference and the teams that were within eight wins away from the eighth seed of the playoffs were allowed to take part in this Bubble, and attendance would be extremely limited in order to minimize the risk of spreading the virus. And because the Lakers were the leaders in the West before the season was suspended, Davis and his teammates needed to prepare for the upcoming continuation of the season, which was set to commence during the latter portion of July.

"I got so fat. I was eating burgers every day," Davis said. "Conditioning is down. I feel 100% healthy. Well, I don't *feel*, I *am*. I feel like I'm ready, ready to go."[xi]

Of course, while the Lakers were still preparing for the continuation of the season, everyone on the team worked hard. Frank Vogel also believed that they had the chance to do something special in the Bubble, especially because he had one of the most special players in the entire league playing at 100% in terms of his health. And it was clear that the time off was great for Davis's overall mental and physical health because he was ready to try to win his first NBA championship.

"Any time Anthony Davis takes the floor, you have a chance to see something special," Vogel said. "He continues to get better and he works extremely hard. Obviously, his talent is off the charts."[xi]

Unlike other players, Davis did not have to wait long to get his mojo back during the Bubble because he was always prepared to score big as long as he was healthy. In his first game in almost five months, he had 34 points in a win over the Los Angeles Clippers. Then, on August 3rd, he dominated the Utah Jazz for 42 points and 12 rebounds. And while the Lakers lost five of their eight games in the Bubble, they were more than ready for the playoffs because Davis and his teammates used the final eight games of the regular season to get back in shape.

At the end of the regular season in the Bubble, Anthony Davis averaged superstar numbers of 26.1 points, 9.3 rebounds, 3.2 assists, and 2.3 blocks while shooting more than 50% from the field. He also led the Lakers in points per game; this was the first time in LeBron James's career that he did not lead his team in scoring! Nevertheless, it was clear that LeBron was comfortable with the fact that AD was the team's leading scorer because this was also the first time in James's career that he led the NBA in assists per game, considering that he had AD as a target inside the paint. Davis also finished second behind Giannis Antetokounmpo for the league's Defensive Player of the Year Award. But it was clear that he was equally deserving of that award because he finished second only to Giannis in terms of defensive win shares and defensive rating out of all of the three finalists for the award.

The reason why Davis was such a good defensive player that season was because he no longer had to do everything by himself. On offense, he did not have to be the one to generate scoring opportunities for the Lakers because LeBron was the one setting the table up for everyone. As such, all that Davis had to do was to pick his spots and learn how to read what his teammates were doing so that he could find an open basket. And whenever he was the focal point of the team's offense, he did not have to play through multiple defenders because his teammates were commanding defensive attention as well.

Of course, his defense was still spot-on because he no longer had to play center throughout an entire game. McGee and Howard were the team's top centers, and that meant that they were asked to be the ones to defend the paint and keep opposing players away from the basket. At the power forward spot, AD was allowed to roam around as a defender because he could patrol the paint to play help defense and block shots from the weak side, or he could cover the perimeter whenever his perimeter defenders collapsed on defense.

Because of AD's insane abilities as a defender, the Lakers were able to finish the season as one of the best defensive teams in the entire league. And his ability to defend was going to be crucial for LA if the team wanted to end what was a unique season with the championship that they had promised to win in Kobe Bryant's memory.

The Lakers met the Blazers in the first round of the playoffs in the Bubble. While Portland surprised LA by drawing first blood, the entire series was in favor of the Lakers. LeBron led the team by averaging a triple-double all series long, but Davis was the most dominant player for the Lakers when it came to his scoring. That was because the Blazers did not have anyone that could match up with him.

Wenyen Gabriel was too small to play physical with him. Meanwhile, the duo of Hassan Whiteside and Jusuf Nurkić were too slow to keep up with him. As such, AD averaged 29.8 points and 9.4 rebounds in five games against the Blazers. The closeout game of the series was his best performance because he went for 43 points while missing only 4 of the 18 shots that he took.

The second-round matchup was literally the worst for the Houston Rockets because they faced a Lakers team that had the advantage in terms of size and athleticism. While Houston won Game 1 of that series, it was apparent that the Lakers were going to make the necessary adjustments to make the matchup favorable for them. And Davis was the key player in that adjustment.

Houston made use of four perimeter players and one undersized big man who could stretch the floor. This allowed the Rockets to have great perimeter shooting while opening the paint up for James Harden and Russell Westbrook to drive and make plays for others. While that strategy would have worked if the Lakers decided to stay big by giving McGee and Howard heavy minutes, it backfired on the Rockets. Davis was now allowed to play heavy minutes at the center spot because he was the only Laker big man who could keep up with the guards of the Rockets while making life hard for Houston's undersized frontline.

Because of that lopsided matchup in favor of the Lakers, the series was over in just five games. After a subpar first game, Davis dominated the series and shot 60% from the field while averaging 25.4 points and 12.4 rebounds. No Rockets player could match up with him inside the paint. And the Rockets could not even make use of their speed and outside shooting because AD could cover the perimeter as well due to his length and mobility as a big man.

The win over the Rockets catapulted the Lakers into the Western Conference Finals, where they met a talented and rising Denver Nuggets team that had triumphed through two straight seven-game series whilst coming back from a 3-1 deficit in both of them. But while the Nuggets were gritty, they were yet to become the championship contenders they would eventually become. And it was obvious that the Lakers had the advantage against Denver in that series.

After the Lakers won Game 1 decisively with Davis going for 37 points, they were in for a fight in Game 2. The Denver Nuggets gave their all in that second game and even went up by a single point during the dying seconds of the game. However, Davis channeled his inner Kobe. In an inbound play with 2.1 seconds to spare, AD got the ball on the left wing and then immediately went for a three-point shot with Jokić's outstretched arms contesting it. But the shot found the bottom of the net as Davis yelled "Kobe" upon making the game-winning shot. This was the shot that eventually set the pace for the entire Lakers team in that playoff run.

Denver managed to win Game 3. But the Lakers simply had too much talent for the Nuggets to overcome. Davis was far better than any other power forward or center that the Nuggets could put on him on the defensive end. Meanwhile, the Lakers had Howard defending Jokic well enough down on the low block. As such, AD was allowed to go all-out on the offensive end by going for 31.2 points on 54.3% shooting from the floor the entire series. Los Angeles went on to qualify for the 2020 NBA Finals after defeating Denver in five games. Overall, the Lakers lost only three games in that run to the championship series.

In the Finals, the Miami Heat were waiting, they were worthy challengers. The Heat were seemingly inspired after somehow defeating all the championship favorites in the Eastern Conference. Jimmy Butler was playing his best brand of basketball, and Bam Adebayo provided enough spark as a second option and a great defensive asset.

This series against the Heat was supposed to be more challenging for Davis and the Lakers because Miami's Adebayo was a much better defender than any of the other defenders that AD had faced in the West. In short, Bam had the body, size, length, and mobility to keep up with him. That was why it was clear that Davis needed to make some adjustments in that series. And while he was the best scorer for the Lakers all postseason long, Los Angeles needed to look at LeBron as the one to lead the team to the promised land.

The first two games of the 2020 Finals were distinctly in favor of the Lakers. Despite Bam's efforts to keep up with AD, the Brow went for an average of 33 points and 11.5 rebounds in both those wins. But when the Heat started denying Davis his touches and made it difficult for him to get the ball in places where he was comfortable, Miami was able to find a way to make the series a bit more challenging. Cue LeBron James, who would step up to carry more of the load.

Miami went on to win two of the next three games to force Game 6. But it was in Game 6 that the Lakers' talent and hunger ultimately triumphed.

LeBron went for a triple-double in that outing. Meanwhile, AD had 10 points and 15 hard-earned rebounds to win his first NBA championship.

While there was no crowd in attendance to celebrate the championship within the Orlando Bubble, this was a sweet moment for a man who had always struggled with success in the NBA from the team perspective. But Anthony Davis could now call himself a champion after what was a unique and eventful 2019-20 season. And he and his teammates were able to deliver a championship months after the untimely passing of one of the franchise's biggest winners, Kobe Bryant, ultimately making good on their promise to honor their fallen comrade.

Davis averaged 25 points and 10.7 rebounds in that series against the Heat. Of course, LeBron went on to win the Finals MVP because of his incredible performance during that championship series. But while AD was not the MVP, he was clearly the instrumental presence that James needed because AD anchored the defense and provided the inside toughness that any championship team needed. Of course, the best part was that Davis was the team's leading scorer all postseason long, proving that he was not just James' sidekick but was a clear partner that was just as important as any other Laker player on that team.

This championship win for Davis also proved another very notable point—that he had the ability to help his team get to the promised land and win the grandest basketball trophy in the entire world as long as he was healthy. After all, his health was always the biggest issue he had faced throughout his entire career. There were more than a few moments in the past wherein his Pelicans team may have had a chance to compete further but failed to do so partly because of Davis's injuries.

But because he was healthy during that championship run and did not miss a single game in the postseason, Davis showed that perhaps his best ability of all was his availability. And he proved himself a true winner after winning an NBA championship to become one of the few players active in the league at that time to win a national championship in college and a ring in the NBA.

Unfortunately for the Lakers, the COVID-19 pandemic prevented them from celebrating with their fans. There was no championship parade in LA because of the pandemic restrictions. As such, the one thing that fans now wanted was to see the Lakers repeating as champions so that they could celebrate with their team and clinch a tie-breaking 18th championship banner. And while LeBron was always going to be a constant threat and contributor for the Lakers, everything boiled down to how healthy and ready AD was going to be for the future of the Lakers, especially now that he had proven that he was more than worth the assets the organization had given up to acquire him.

Injury-Plagued Seasons

After the successful 2019-20 campaign, the Lakers only had a few months to rest because the 2020-2021 season started in December of 2020. Meanwhile, it was only in October of 2020 that they had won their title in the Bubble. LA only had a little over two months to rest and prepare for the next season. And that was not entirely good news on the part of the core duo of the Lakers.

Even though Davis had committed to the Lakers by re-signing with the team for a five-year sum worth $190 million, the ever-present concern was that he had a history of injuries. He stayed healthy throughout the 2019-20 season and was able to play all of the Lakers' postseason games in the Bubble. But history suggested that Davis was probably not going to stay healthy for long because the wear and tear that his body goes through tends to be heavier compared to many other players due to his playing style.

Meanwhile, LeBron was already 36 years old and was not getting any younger. The Lakers also lost key pieces during the offseason. So, while LA was still a contender for the championship, the Lakers had to endure several challenges along the way throughout the 2020-21 season if they wanted to repeat as champions.

The addition of new players allowed Davis to rest a bit on the offensive end. Montrezl Harrell, the NBA's reigning sixth man of the year, provided some spark off the bench. Dennis Schröder also performed well at the point guard spot by providing timely shots from the perimeter. As such, AD did not have to be too assertive on the offensive end because he had players who could cover some of the areas on that part of the game. His defense was still spot-on for the Lakers.

But there was another big problem that the Lakers faced in relation to Anthony Davis. The season was shortened to 72 games to make up for the fact that it started late. However, the schedule was compressed to speed the regular season up. This meant that there were more back-to-back games for every team in the league. And the problem for the Lakers specifically was that Davis did not get much rest before the start of the regular season.

The Lakers rested Davis when there were back-to-back games to make sure that he was going to stay healthy during the regular season. His minutes were also managed well enough to decrease the load on his body. But that did not matter because he still ended up getting injured during one of the most important parts of the regular season.

Davis missed 30 straight games, the longest absence of his entire career, due to calf and heel issues. He became inactive on February 14, 2021, and was only able to return on April 22nd. LeBron also faced his own series of injuries and was only able to play 45 games during the 2020-21 regular season.

So, despite entering the season as defending champions, the Lakers looked vulnerable because they did not have their two best players throughout a good part of the regular season. Before Davis and James got injured, the Lakers had a good shot at locking up the top seed in the West. But while the two best players on the team were absent, the other guys were able to find a way to compete. And the Lakers' top-rated defense allowed them to stay afloat all season long despite the fact that their two best players were nursing injuries.

Upon Davis's return, the Lakers won their last four games and were looking like championship contenders once again. The superstar big man went for a season-high 42 points in a win over the Phoenix Suns on May 9th. It seemed like nothing was going to stop him and his team from making a huge splash in the playoffs, despite entering the postseason with the seventh seed in the West after defeating the Golden State Warriors in the 2021 Play-In Tournament. Davis averaged lower numbers of 21.8 points, 7.9 rebounds, and 3.1 assists while shooting a career-low 49.1% from the field.

The fact that Davis had an uncharacteristically inefficient season was surprising. In fact, this was his most inefficient season ever since his rookie year. It was due to the fact that he had changed his game up a bit to address the problems he was facing with his injuries. To decrease the wear and tear on his body, he was more of a shooter that season. He only shot 24.3% of his field-goal attempts from within three feet of the basket. Most of his shots were jump shots that he took from midrange.

While AD was always capable of shooting jumpers, he was never the most efficient jump shooter in the game. Davis's jump shot was almost always just a complementary aspect of his ability to dominate the paint because defenses would rather allow him to shoot jumpers than give him space to drive and score easy points near the basket. But his jump shot was never his best weapon. And when defenses realized that he was more inclined to patrol the perimeter that season, they adjusted by making it hard for him to shoot efficient jump shots.

As such, there were questions about whether or not he could still be the Anthony Davis of old, the man who had dominated during the 2020 Playoffs with a good mix of inside scoring and perimeter shooting. He was now more concerned with preserving his body by shooting jumpers because he understood that his best ability was always his availability. To stay available, he had to stay healthy, and that meant becoming more of a shooter. And this became an issue during the 2021 postseason, despite the fact that the Lakers had a chance to actually defend their hard-earned 2020 Championship.

In the first round, the defending champions went up against the Phoenix Suns, who were hungry to finally make some noise in the playoffs after going undefeated in the eight games that they played during the 2020 Bubble games in Orlando. The Suns even won Game 1 to make the Lakers realize that they were serious enough in their quest to unseat LA as the kings of the West early on. But Davis dominated the Suns' frontline in the next two games by averaging 34 points, 10.5 rebounds, 3.5 assists, and 2 blocks in Games 2 and 3. He led the Lakers to a 2-1 series lead over the Suns as it was clear that this team was still the defending champion.

Unfortunately, in Game 4, Davis suffered a strained groin that kept him out of the entire bout. The Lakers lost by eight points, and it was obvious that having AD would have changed the outcome of that game because he was the team's best defensive presence. Davis also missed Game 5, which was a massive blowout loss for the Lakers. The Suns were now up 3-2 in the series and looking to eliminate the Lakers in Game 6.

After missing Game 5, Davis tried to keep the championship hopes alive by making himself available to play in Game 6. But he only played five minutes before re-aggravating his injury. The Lakers ended up losing that game to bow out of the playoffs in only six bouts against the Phoenix Suns. And it was clear that Davis's presence was the aspect that the Lakers missed the most in that series against the Suns due to the fact that his availability was always the barometer of success for that team.

There was no arguing against the fact that LeBron James was still the team's best player because he was the favorite to win the MVP award before he went down with his own injury. But while it was true that he was the team's top option on offense and the best facilitator on that squad, it was Davis's presence that provided the inside toughness the team needed on both ends of the floor. The Lakers needed AD just as much as that team needed James. And that was the reason why everyone knew they were never going to compete for a championship without Davis being at his healthiest.

The need for another star to help carry the team whenever LeBron and AD were out was one of the things that the Lakers looked at during the offseason. Despite how capable Kyle Kuzma and Kentavious Caldwell-Pope were at picking up the slack without the team's best players, they were the ones who needed to be traded to get another star to LA. Thus, the Lakers made a move that sent those two role players to the Washington Wizards to acquire Russell

Westbrook, who had just come off averaging a triple-double for the fourth time in five seasons.

But the most important aspect of that Westbrook trade was the roster setup. Russell Westbrook thrived in an offense that allowed him to have the ball in his hands so that he could make plays for others. He lacked the outside shooting of some of the other point guards in the league but his athleticism and ability to get to the basket were still there, despite his comparatively advanced age in basketball years. And he was known for finishing strong near the basket or making plays for others whenever he broke defenses down.

However, the problem was that it was evident from the very start that Westbrook's abilities were not made for the Lakers. That was because the team's offense still started and ended with LeBron James. Any team that had LeBron would always run the offense through him because he is arguably the greatest of all time at generating points for himself and his teammates with his scoring and passing abilities. Meanwhile, Russell Westbrook's role on the teams he had played for was exactly the same role that James played for the Lakers. Thus, it was an awkward fit from day one. Plus, while Westbrook was a sure-fire Hall-of-Famer and one of the greatest players the league has ever seen, he was already past his prime.

But perhaps the worst part was that neither James nor Westbrook were known to be great off-ball players. While they could hit jumpers from time to time, neither of them was a consistent shooter. And they were not even great at cutting to the basket as off-ball options.

Of course, Anthony Davis was the only great off-ball player on that Lakers team. He was an excellent option for either James or Westbrook because of his pick-and-roll abilities and his unstoppable finishing skills near the basket.

But the team needed spacing for AD to be effective. And because neither James nor Westbrook was known for spacing the ball effectively, it was going to be more difficult for Davis to find easy baskets inside the paint without having multiple defenders on him.

The adjustment period was obviously going to be long because these three players needed to learn how to play together to maximize the chances of the Lakers to win another championship.

Davis, of course, was healthy enough to start the regular season playing one of his best brands of basketball. He continued being one of the team's barometers for success as he went for 35 points and 17 rebounds in a win over the San Antonio Spurs on October 26, 2021. In a win over the Hornets on November 8th, he had 32 points, 12 rebounds, 3 steals, and 5 blocks. And in another win over the Spurs, he dominated his way to 34 points and 15 rebounds.

Davis impressed people well enough that season as he played 27 out of the Lakers' first 30 games. He looked pretty healthy during the earlier part of the 2021-22 season. But while that may have been true, there were problems that needed to be addressed in relation to the way he played the game. The fact of the matter was, the Lakers were barely hanging on during that part of the season.

Davis was always known for his ability to shoot jumpers for a power forward that stands nearly seven feet tall and with a wingspan of an eagle. But, unlike the previous season, he was no longer shooting a lot of jumpers because he needed to stay close to the basket now that he was once against playing center for the team. And whenever AD took his game away from the paint, it just looked ugly.

Davis was shooting around 37.6% of his shots within three feet from the basket, and this number was clearly higher than the 24.3% that he averaged a year ago. Davis still played out on the perimeter from time to time because it added a dimension to his game. But while he was shooting nearly 80% from the field whenever he scored the ball from within three feet of the basket, the numbers dropped whenever he took shots at least 5 feet from the goal. In fact, during the early part of the season, Davis was the most inefficient jump shooter in the entire NBA, even though he was actually known for hitting jump shots better than most big men.[xii]

The issue was not that Davis's ability to shoot had diminished. Instead, there were several other factors that the Lakers needed to address. The spacing was so bad because no one on that team could shoot jumpers on a regular basis. Hence, Davis did not have the luxury of space to shoot jumpers efficiently. Defenders were often right in his face whenever he was out on the perimeter. The opposing teams could now allow defenders to stay tight on Davis wherever he was on the floor due to the fact that they could send an extra help defender near the basket whenever AD drove.

In the past, Davis could shoot jumpers efficiently because he was dared to shoot. Defenses were afraid of his ability to drive because no one was going to be near the basket to help his defender when there were multiple shooters spacing the floor. But during the 2021-22 season, defenders that were tasked to guard a non-shooter like Westbrook could cheat on defense and stay close to the basket to help cover Davis's or LeBron's man whenever they gave their defensive assignments space to drive.

As such, because Davis's man was almost always allowed to stay close to him, there were a lot of instances wherein AD needed to fade or shoot a contested jumper from the perimeter. Those were never efficient shots for him because most of his efficient jump shots were made whenever defenses were giving him space to shoot because they were afraid of his ability to get to the basket.

To make things worse, Davis ended up spraining his MCL on December 17th in a loss to the Minnesota Timberwolves. He missed a total of 17 straight games. The Lakers, meanwhile, were 7-10 in those games he missed. Because of his injury, Davis was not an All-Star for the first time in eight years. And after playing 10 games since returning from the MCL sprain, he went on to miss an additional 18 straight games due to an ankle sprain that he suffered in a win over the Utah Jazz on February 16, 2022.

The Lakers went on to lose 15 of the 18 games that Davis missed. Unlike the prior season when the Lakers were still able to weather the storm despite missing James and AD a lot during the regular season, this team was not built for that kind of challenge because the roster makeup was not exactly good outside of the team's star trio. And Westbrook, for all his talents, just did not fit with that team.

Thus, the Lakers ended up with a record of 33-49 at the end of the regular season. Anthony Davis averaged 23.2 points, 9.9 rebounds, and 2.3 blocks. But he missed over half of the entire season due to injuries. His absences hurt the Lakers, who could not weather the storm with Westbrook leading the team whenever AD and LeBron were out. As such, the team missed the playoffs for the first time since Davis was traded to the Lakers.

Return to Elite Form

After what was obviously a failed season on the part of the Lakers, the team decided to run things back with the same group of players but with a new coach in the form of Darvin Ham. This did not seem like the best decision because any head coach would struggle if they had a roster clogged up with players who did not gel well with one another, no matter how talented they might be individually. But the most critical part for the Lakers was to make sure that their best players were healthy, including Anthony Davis.

Davis started the season healthy and was putting up good numbers, but the team was still struggling to win games. The problems with spacing had gone unresolved and carried over from the previous season, and the Lakers were forced to shoot outside shots by opposing defenses because opponents would rather gamble on LA's poor outside shooting instead of allowing the trio of James, Davis, and Westbrook to get easy buckets inside the paint. This led to a dismal 2-12 record early on, and Davis was not particularly assertive in that stretch of games.

One of the biggest criticisms about Davis's game was that he lacked the same kind of assertiveness and aggression that he had displayed when he was still playing in New Orleans. Back in the Big Easy, he owned the offense and was so aggressive on the offensive end that many people believed he was the most talented power forward the league has ever seen.

While Davis was still at the top of the list in terms of talent at the power forward and center spots, the last few seasons in LA were indicative of the fact that he was no longer the best power forward in the league. He was becoming a bit too passive on offense and was more likely to settle for jumpers instead of attacking the basket. And while injuries played a big role in Davis's lack of aggression, the team's makeup was also a significant factor.

The Lakers had given up talented players in a trade to bring Davis to Los Angeles. He was supposedly going to take a huge load off LeBron's shoulders on the offensive end. That was because AD is almost a decade younger than James and has all the talent and skill to be the top offensive option on any team. But, with the exception of the 2019-20 season, AD became notably passive for someone who has the immense talent and skill level that he possesses. This led some critics to speculate that he needed to be more assertive while he was on the floor because the Lakers needed him to be at his best if they wanted to compete for a playoff spot.

To that end, AD cut the jump shots and decided to play like a true freakish big man. During a day and age that only had a few true centers who played big and could still keep up with faster players, Davis stood out. He could dominate smaller centers on small-ball lineups but could also outrun and outpace bigger centers that were not built to have his mobility and athleticism.

So, even though the Lakers lacked the proper spacing to allow him to dominate inside the paint without having multiple defenders draped all over him, Davis started to become more assertive out of necessity. He understood that his team was not going anywhere with him playing the more passive role he had fallen into.

From November 13th to the 22nd, the Brow went for four straight games of scoring 30 or more points. He averaged 35.5 points, 18.3 rebounds, 2.3 steals, and 2.5 blocks while shooting over 62% from the field during that stretch.

It was clear that he understood what he needed to do for the Lakers because that squad needed a big man who was playing like a true big man during an era that only had a handful of big men that could match up with him. He was not only scoring assertively inside the paint but was also collecting rebounds at the highest level possible in his entire career.

On December 2nd, Davis went for 44 points and 10 rebounds in a win over the Milwaukee Bucks and even outplayed Giannis Antetokounmpo, who many people believed was what AD *should* have been if he was not being too passive on the offensive end. And just two days later, he proved how unstoppable he was by going for 55 points and 17 rebounds in a win over the Washington Wizards.

Through his first 25 games, Davis averaged 27.4 points, 12.1 rebounds, and 2.1 blocks while shooting a ridiculous clip of 59.4% from the field. The reason why he was able to return to his elite form and look better than ever was the fact that he was no longer trying to be "friendly" with his approach as a player. AD banged with big men inside the paint, pushed smaller players around using his strength and heft, and fought for possessions consistently. In fact, he became an unstoppable inside presence that season by limiting his shot attempts to within 10 feet of the basket. Indeed, only 32.8% of his shot attempts were from beyond 10 feet. A year ago, that number was 42.3%! During the 2020-21 season, over half of his shots came from 10 feet or beyond.

Because Davis was now taking the shots that he knew were his most efficient, he was putting up great numbers on a poor team that still needed outside shooting from its guards. Davis was doing his part by averaging 65.1% shooting from within 10 feet of the basket, as he was essentially an automatic bucket whenever he had the ball inside the paint.

But, then again, injuries were constants that Anthony Davis struggled with his entire career. It did not matter whether he was playing aggressively or passively because injuries always seemed to find a way to get to him. He was no longer playing the same passive style that he was playing the previous two years, but his body still struggled to stay healthy no matter what he did.

Davis missed all of the Lakers' games from December 18, 2022, to January 25, 2023, due to a foot injury—a total of 20 straight games during that stretch. And while it may be true that he got injured, he did not try to baby his injury because he continued to play a more aggressive style of basketball.

Of course, his dominance was lost in all of the things that were happening to the Lakers that season. LeBron James was at the center of all the attention that year because he eventually passed Kareem Abdul-Jabbar as the NBA's leader in career points scored. Meanwhile, the Lakers were also being mocked by critics and analysts because they had struggled to win games and were on their way to the lottery. But while all that may be true, Davis helped to turn the season around for the Lakers.

Before the trade deadline, the Lakers shook the entire roster by trading away some of the pieces that did not fit that team. This included Russell Westbrook, who was sent to the Utah Jazz, who waived him. Russ found a home with the LA Clippers. But the moves that the Lakers made allowed them to bring in other talented players who helped LeBron and AD. This included Rui Hachimura, Jarred Vanderbilt, and D'Angelo Russell. These shrewd changes finally allowed the Lakers to compete hard during the latter portion of the regular season. Of course, Anthony Davis feasted well enough now that he had players who could help him and James.

On March 7th, AD went for 30 points and 22 rebounds in a win over the Memphis Grizzlies. A week later, he dominated the Pelicans with 35 points and 17 rebounds. Then, from March 29th to April 2nd, he led his team to three straight wins by averaging 38.7 points and 11.7 rebounds. Thanks to the Lakers' roster shakeup, they were able to help their best players lead the team back to playoff contention.

At the age of 29, Davis averaged 25.9 points while shooting a new career high of 56.3% from the field. He also averaged a new career high of 12.5 rebounds. There was good reason to believe that AD would have made both the All-NBA and All-Defensive teams had he been healthy enough to play more games. He missed a total of 26 games that season. That number sounds significant, but that was enough to still be seen as progress for him, considering that he has had such a long history of injuries.

The Lakers had the NBA's best record ever since the trade deadline, and that was how they were able to sneak their way into the Play-In Tournament, wherein they secured the seventh seed in the West by defeating the Minnesota Timberwolves in overtime. This win allowed the Lakers to match up with an upstart and somewhat cocky Memphis Grizzlies team that was also facing its own fair share of controversies.

Against a team that struggled with its own off-court issues, Davis was able to dominate. He helped the Lakers win Game 1 when he finished with 22 points, 12 rebounds, and 7 blocks. The Grizzlies won Game 2, but they lost the entire series because Dillon Brooks of Memphis decided to talk trash to LeBron James. This set the tone for the entire series, as the Grizzlies added fuel to a fire that they were not ready to extinguish.

In Game 3, Davis led the way with 31 points and 17 rebounds. He did not have the best scoring game in Game 4 but he contributed on the defensive end with 4 blocks. The Grizzlies survived to win Game 5. But the Lakers eventually won the series in six games by winning Game 6 by 40 big points. Davis ended the first round with 16 points, 14 rebounds, and 5 blocks in that closeout game. He averaged 20.8 points, 13.7 rebounds, and 4.3 blocks against the Grizzlies in that series.

While AD was not the best scorer in that first-round matchup with Memphis, what was clear was that he was willing to do everything on the defensive end. He decided to own the paint like he was protecting his house from armed robbers. Davis was blocking shots left and right and making it hard for Ja Morant and the other Grizzlies to invade his space inside the paint. He made use of his length, timing, mobility, and athleticism to dominate the paint in that series. And that was because AD knew that he could trust LeBron and his other teammates to deliver and do their part on the offensive end as well.

Davis continued to play the role of an old-school inside presence for the Lakers in their second-round matchup with the Golden State Warriors, as old rivals in LeBron James and Stephen Curry were ready to renew the biggest rivalry of the 2010s. And while the two most influential players of that era were all over the headlines, the one player whom the Warriors were more concerned with than any other Laker was Anthony Davis because he was far too dominant for any of the Golden State big men to contain inside the paint. And AD made sure to stamp his dominance all over that series by going for 30 points, 23 rebounds, and 4 blocks in a win over the Warriors in Game 1.

The Warriors tried their best to neutralize Davis's defensive abilities in that series. It was as if he was prime Bill Russell with the way that Golden State was more concerned with his ability to cover the basket than any of the other Lakers' ability to score. But none of what the Warriors did worked to keep AD out of the paint.

The Lakers lost Game 2 but got a quick 3-1 advantage with wins in Games 3 and 4. Davis averaged double-doubles in those games and was a presence inside the paint with his ability to defend everyone on the Warriors' roster. And though the Warriors forced Game 6, Davis simply owned the paint by going for 17 points and 20 rebounds to defeat the defending champions in six games.

Anthony Davis was nothing short of a monster in that series against the Warriors. He did not score a lot of points to put the defending champions away. But what was clear was that his defensive impact on the floor was similar to how old-school big men were supposed to affect an NBA game. He kept smaller players out of the paint, grabbed all the rebounds, and asserted his size over the undersized Warriors frontline.

Davis averaged 21.5 points, 14.5 rebounds, 3.3 assists, 1.5 steals, and 2.2 blocks in that series against the defending champions. And while he did not score many points, he was arguably the most crucial player on the part of the Lakers because of how he anchored the defense.

The Lakers were now back in the Western Conference Finals nearly three years since they had won the championship in the Orlando Bubble. They were also facing familiar opponents in the form of the Denver Nuggets, whom they had defeated in five games nearly three years ago. But this Denver team was an entirely different version of the squad that the Lakers defeated back in the Bubble. Nikola Jokić had transformed into one of the greatest offensive options the league had ever seen. Jamal Murray was on a mission to make his comeback season a Cinderella run. And the role players on that team all had the ability to play off the stellar abilities of their star duo.

Anthony Davis's biggest challenge was to keep Jokić outside of the paint because he averaged over 63% from the field that season, despite taking tough shots inside the paint. But the most daunting aspect of his game was that the Joker could make plays for others when his ability to make shots was neutralized. He almost became only the third player in league history to average a triple-double because he was capable of giving easy looks to his teammates, despite playing the center position. And it was also the fact that opposing players were afraid of Jokić's ability to make plays for others that made him difficult to cover because setting an extra defender on him meant that he could find the player left wide-open by the help defense.

In truth, no one could fault Davis for how Jokić was able to methodically destroy that Lakers team. The Lakers big man tried his best to keep him out of the paint and cover his shots. Davis even had great games all series long. In fact, in Game 1, he had 40 points and 10 rebounds. But the Joker was far too difficult for any one player to cover.

In Game 1, as the third-quarter clock was winding down, Jokić brought the ball up the court and had no option but to step back and launch a high-arching, 29-foot three-pointer over the 7'5" wingspan of Anthony Davis. As the shot found the bottom of the net, the only thing that AD could do was look at the opposing center and smile at him in disbelief. In Game 3, the Joker made another similar shot by stepping back and hitting a one-legged fading three-pointer over Davis's arm. And when he was not hitting impossible shots, he was making plays for others.

In the end, the Nuggets simply outplayed the Lakers to win the series in four games. Both Jokić and Jamal Murray methodically destroyed their superstar counterparts in that series, especially with the Joker averaging a triple-double. Denver went on to the NBA Finals, where they won it all against the Miami Heat.

In retrospect, there was no shame in the fact that the Lakers simply lost to the superior team. And, in Anthony Davis's case, he was quick to learn that there

117

were other big men who were dominating the NBA in an entirely different way compared to how he dominated the league himself.

Even though the Lakers lost in the Western Conference Finals, they achieved more than what most people ever thought they could accomplish that season. Just a few months prior, the Lakers were seemingly well out of playoff contention, and the only reason for Lakers fans to be happy was the fact that LeBron James broke Kareem Abdul-Jabbar's record for career points scored. But LA turned the season around after the trade deadline. And the return of Anthony Davis, who sparked the team's defense during the playoffs, made a championship run possible for the Lakers.

So, while LA may have failed to get to the Finals, the outlook was bright because this team finally had a roster that was built to help LeBron and AD, not hinder them. Of course, while LeBron's title window was closing due to his advanced age, all eyes were on Davis because his health had always been the true barometer of a deep playoff run for the Lakers. So, if Anthony Davis can stay healthy in the next few seasons, another championship run is not out of the conversation.

Chapter 5: Team USA

Before he started his NBA career, and a few months after helping the Kentucky Wildcats win the NCAA National Championship over the Kansas Jayhawks, Anthony Davis was one of the young finalists that officials were looking at to fill a spot on the US men's basketball team that would compete in the 2012 Summer Olympics held in London, England.

AD's invitation to play with Team USA came after there were some injuries to other players, including Dwight Howard. What was interesting about Davis's inclusion in the U.S. roster was that he was the first player since Emeka Okafor in 2004 to play for the red, white, and blue in the Olympics without having any previous professional experience in the NBA. Davis found himself among great names like Blake Griffin, Kevin Love, and Tyson Chandler as some of the prospective post players who were being examined.

There was some concern when Davis suffered a sprained ankle during a workout in June, and there were doubts that he was going to hold off on playing in the Olympics and heal up in time for his impending rookie year in the NBA in the late fall. However, he was selected to the final roster after Griffin had to leave the squad due to a knee injury.

During the 2012 Olympics, Davis mostly played on the bench with the starting five, which included Carmelo Anthony, Kobe Bryant, LeBron James, and Chris Paul. Team USA found themselves in Group A in the preliminary round and went 5-0 to finish at the top of their group before going into the knockout round. In their first game of group play on July 29, 2012, Team USA defeated France, where Davis had only three points from a field goal and a free throw.

Davis saw an increased number of minutes as the tournament continued with 12 points and 3 rebounds in the team's 110-63 win over Tunisia on July 31st. He followed that up with a near double-double, notching nine points and six rebounds in a blowout victory 156-73 over Nigeria on August 2nd. However, Davis did not play in the team's close win over Lithuania on August 4th, and he played only a handful of minutes in the victory over Argentina a few days later. He failed to score during the championship round while Team USA defeated Spain in the gold medal finals, 107-100, on August 12th.

This was not the only international competition experience for Davis, as he also joined Team USA for the International Basketball Federation's (FIBA) 2014 Basketball World Cup played in Spain, which transpired during two weeks in late August and through mid-September. Davis joined a team that featured numerous younger talents from the NBA such as James Harden, Stephen Curry, and Derrick Rose.

In the first game of their Group C play, Davis had 17 points, making 6 out of 8 from the field and all 5 free throws to go along with 4 rebounds in a 114-55 win over Finland on August 30, 2014. Davis scored another 19 points and 6 rebounds to go along with 2 steals and 2 blocks in a win over Turkey on August 31st. Davis scored another 12 points and collected 6 rebounds to help the USA go undefeated in a win over Ukraine on September 4th. That group play record of 5-0 helped them advance to the knockout stage.

Davis had one of his toughest games in the World Cup on September 5, 2014, in the Round of 16. While the USA defeated Mexico 86-63, Davis was two of nine from the field for only two points, but he did have six rebounds, four blocked shots, two steals, and one assist. A few days later on September 9th, Davis got his first double-double in his international career with 13 points and 11 rebounds in a win over Slovenia.

Davis followed that performance up with another 12 points and 6 rebounds to help the USA beat Lithuania in the semifinals. Davis did not have double figures on the box score in the championship finals game with only seven points and four rebounds, as the USA defeated Serbia on September 14th. During that tournament, he averaged 12.3 points and 6.6 rebounds after failing to put up any memorable performances in the 2012 London Olympics.

Chapter 6: Personal Life

Growing up in Englewood, Anthony Davis always imagined himself becoming successful and taking care of his family. He wanted to provide for them and take them out of the dangerous area that they resided in. Even if basketball did not work out for him, he was always thinking long-term—he also envisioned himself working as a high school teacher or in PT. Growing up in a rough neighborhood can truly impact your life. You can either succumb to the environment in which you live, or you can rise above it and choose your destiny. Fortunately, Davis opted for the latter and started working hard in both his academics and athletics.

His most expensive purchase made after signing his rookie contract was buying his parents a large house. Anthony remembered the sacrifices, hard work, and dedication that his parents had always put forth to raise him the way they did. The only way to repay them was to make sure that they were set for life. He bought them a house and a nice car so that they lived comfortably. Davis remembered the days in which they only had a small Dodge as their car and how his parents had invested in a truck so that Davis was comfortable when they traveled with the team. Davis bought his parents an SUV so that there would be enough room to fit all of them when his family came to visit.

Davis is a family man and he takes care of them well. Davis also wants to be smart with his money, so he invests it the right way—when he leaves the game, he wants to be financially stable so that he never has to worry about his money running out.

In a recent interview, Anthony shared stories of friends and family that he had not seen or talked to in a long time. Many of them were asking for favors, both financially and socially. The majority of family members reached out to his grandmother and she dealt with them accordingly, often without notifying Anthony so that he would not be distracted.

In some instances, friends asked for a shout-out on Twitter or Instagram so that people would ask them how they knew Davis. In other cases, they were simply hoping that Anthony would share his hard-earned success with them in some way. However, AD was a smart kid and knew that they were mostly looking for frivolous favors. Thus, he often just ignored their calls and went about his business.

As a child growing up in Englewood, Anthony was surrounded by many distractions that could jeopardize his future, but nevertheless, he managed to stay out of trouble and avoid the peer pressure that is so often prevalent in disadvantaged communities like his. Instead, Anthony just focused on what his parents emphasized: education.

After being drafted into the NBA, Davis suddenly had more money than he could ever dream of having. And coming from an environment where there was never enough financial security, Anthony is not afraid to admit that he loves money, and he professes that he wants to become a global icon.

In that regard, he wants to become like MJ, Magic, or Kobe, all of whom have invested their money well and are known globally for their shrewd financial endeavors. Davis is very intelligent and is always looking to the future. He knows that his basketball career will not last forever. So, if he wants to provide for his family, he has to make the right decisions.

Anthony's favorite place to shop is Louis Vuitton, and he loves pizza. He is not afraid to claim that the best pizza is in Chicago. However, while Chicago does have some tasty deep-dish pizzas, what Davis is most hungry for is basketball.

Chapter 7: Impact on Basketball

Anthony Davis has had a tremendous impact on the sport of basketball. Not only is he known for his athletic ability and freakish set of skills but he also has been a great role model for kids growing up. Davis is a laid-back, humble player who focuses on education before athletics.

He is also very comfortable in his own skin and has committed to keeping his now-famous unibrow for life. It is not every day that you find someone who has a noticeable trait like that and is comfortable enough not to change it! He has also trademarked a few slogans with regards to his unibrow which he hopes will help him in becoming a global icon, including "Raise the Brow" and "Fear the Brow."

Davis' mentality and outlook on life are at a mature level. He will always be known as the player who shot up eight inches and won an NCAA title and an Olympic Gold medal in his desire to provide for his family. During interviews, you can sense that Davis has it all planned out. He will always have an impact on athletes by inspiring them to think about the future and not be foolish with unnecessary purchases. Anthony knows that money can easily come and go, and that you need to be wise with your financial decisions if you truly want to secure your future.

Concerning what he has done in basketball, Anthony Davis is one of the players who started the unicorn movement. In basketball, unicorns are players who are as tall as centers but with the skillset and athletic abilities of a guard. At over 6'10" and with a near-7'5" wingspan, Anthony Davis was a physical freak, especially now that he has matured into his body and weighs over 250 pounds. However, what made him a special unicorn was the fact that he could run the floor like a small forward, bring the ball down like a guard, and jump through the roof like Dominique Wilkins.

What makes a unicorn special in today's NBA is how versatile they are. The league has steadily been transitioning to a pace-and-space style that utilizes smaller and faster players for more spacing and speed. Because of that, some small forwards are asked to move up a position while traditional power forwards play as undersized centers. Yet, because unicorns are both big and versatile, teams have the luxury of playing them at different positions without losing size, athleticism, or shooting. On Davis's part, his size and length allow him to play the center spot while retaining the same kind of defensive intensity and offensive versatility he displays whenever he plays the power forward position.

Before Anthony Davis made the jump to the NBA, there was no player other than Kevin Durant who had the same physical capabilities and athletic skillset. Since then, there have been several players who have gone on to become unicorns themselves.

At 6'11", Giannis Antetokounmpo may have the height and length of a center but he moves around the court like a point guard. Meanwhile, the 7'3" Kristaps Porzingis has the skills of a Dirk Nowitzki but the mobility of a small forward. All those players are considered some of the best unicorns in the league. Anthony Davis is a headliner in that regard.

More importantly, Anthony Davis's rise as an elite superstar is also one of the ways he impacted basketball. Seen as a raw prospect with freakish physical tools and athletic capabilities, Davis, as a rookie, was far from the player that he would become. However, everybody knew that he had the potential to become great. He was not a Kevin Garnett, who already showed flashes of his diverse skillset back in high school. Nor was he Kevin Durant, who was already a scoring savant in his collegiate season.

Instead, Anthony Davis was merely a great finisher around the basket. Teams were expecting him to improve as a post player to become a better version of Tyson Chandler. However, Davis exceeded expectations in the blink of an eye. From being a mere rim finisher, he suddenly improved not only his play down at the low post but also his abilities as a ball-handler and as a shooter. AD began hitting the mid-range shot like he was a shooting guard and also started to take his man off the dribble from the perimeter like he was a point guard.

Of course, while Davis developed the skill set of a great all-around big man, he returned to the basics of what a big man should do by dominating the paint on both ends of the court. With his size and length, he became an unstoppable force near the basket because not a lot of power forwards and centers could match up with him physically. Today, he is so much longer and stronger than most other power forwards in the NBA. And opposing centers do not have the speed to keep up with his mobility.

On the defensive end, he can play the role of a prime Bill Russell by using his mobile feet to cover enough ground to defend the basket at any given time. While most power forwards and centers would rather wait near the paint to become effective defensive players, Anthony Davis had the ability to cover the perimeter but recover just in time to bother or block a shot near the basket with his speed, agility, and athleticism.

With the way that Anthony Davis exceeded expectations, he has become an inspiration for younger players who are underdogs and never expected to become more than what they already were in college. Davis defied scouting reports by working hard to transform himself. From an elite finisher and versatile defensive force, he became one of the best scorers in the entire NBA because of his diverse set of skills. By working hard every season, he has shown that you can indeed become more than the sum of your parts.

Chapter 8: Legacy and Future

Anthony Davis carries with him the legacy of some of the greatest big men to ever play the game. The power forward has become today's NBA premier big man, not only because of how the league has been utilizing frontcourt players at a lesser rate but also because frankly—AD is just that good. Davis is the ideal superstar to carry the banner of some of the best legends who have trod the court before him, and he does so in style.

Seemingly molded in the shape of Kevin Garnett because of his physical tools, Anthony Davis came into the NBA with the athletic capabilities of a taller Karl Malone but with a potential that could challenge the legends of Tim Duncan and Dirk Nowitzki. Some would say that it's crazy to compare Anthony Davis to those legends, but he does have the talent and skill to someday belong in the same category. When the dust settles we could easily see Davis as one of the best power forwards in league history.

Standing over 6'10" with a wingspan of about 7'5" and weighing well over 250 pounds at his peak, Anthony Davis seemed like the second coming of Kevin Garnett because of the athletic versatility he had at his size. However, he became so much more than that. With the added strength Davis got from weight training, he began finishing pick-and-rolls like Karl Malone. He trained himself to learn the same post moves that made Tim Duncan one of the greatest of all time. And to punctuate all of that, Davis developed a jump shot that made defenses give him the same respect as Dirk Nowitzki out on the perimeter. And, if that were not enough, he could even put the ball down on the floor like he was Charles Barkley. Yes, he is just that good.

With a diverse set of skills that make him look like the perfect mash-up of yesteryear's best power forwards, Davis carries the legacy and the flag that has been passed on from the likes of Malone, Barkley, Duncan, Garnett, and Nowitzki. As far as talent and star potential are concerned, he indeed has the makings to follow in their footsteps and might someday even be considered better than all of them.

As the New Orleans Pelican's former premier superstar and former face of their franchise, Anthony Davis might arguably already be the best player in the history of that team. There have only been a few superstars that have played for New Orleans in the franchise's brief history, but that does not take anything away from what Davis accomplished for the team in such a short span of time.

In less than 500 games played for the team, he became the franchise's all-time leader in points, rebounds, and blocks. And he did that despite having played fewer games and seasons than Chris Paul and David West, who are two of the best players the franchise has seen.

Proving that he is indeed a defensive stalwart, Anthony Davis is also second all-time in steals and is trailing only Chris Paul in that regard. After playing six seasons for the team, he had shattered all of the records previously set by Chris Paul and David West except assists and steals, which still belong to CP3.

Davis has already made himself the best player in franchise history during his stay with the team. Failing to win a title in the Big Easy and leaving the New Orleans Pelicans in favor of the Los Angeles Lakers has not changed that fact. No other player in franchise history has ever been able to do what Davis could on both ends of the floor.

Anthony Davis can now be regarded as both the present and the future of the Los Angeles Lakers. Playing alongside a proven winner like LeBron James has boosted his ability to win games. And because Davis is now playing with a fellow superstar whom he gels well with, he has seen better shots and efficiency numbers because he no longer has to carry the offense on his own and is allowed to focus more on doing what needs to be done to win the game.

Still one of the better big men in the league, Anthony Davis has room to grow as a player and leader as well. He has already proven himself a winner by helping the Los Angeles Lakers win a record-tying 17th NBA championship in 2020. While he was not the best player on that team, he proved that he was just as important as LeBron James was to the team's success because he was a matchup nightmare for all the other opposing players. And his defense always stood out.

Davis carries not only the hopes of a franchise on his broad shoulders but also the legacy of some of the best big men to ever play the game. As the league has been trending toward a perimeter and guard-oriented game, recent championship teams have leaned on the strengths of their perimeter players for their title wins. Big men have only become role players or tertiary players in today's NBA when it comes to building a championship roster. But Davis shows that a big man still has a vital place on a contending NBA team.

Considering that Anthony Davis is the big man's standard-bearer in today's NBA, winning a title meant that power forwards and centers are not yet obsolete when it comes to winning titles. Davis won a championship in 2020 by playing the role of a true big man in the sense that he scored inside baskets and timely perimeter shots while grabbing rebounds and swatting shots. As such, he was indispensable for the Lakers in that 2020 title run. Davis proved that a good championship team could always find value in a dominant superstar big man.

131

With the way that he has evolved as a player, Davis has also redefined the position of the big man. He used to identify himself as a power forward and hated playing center when he was with the New Orleans Pelicans. But with the Lakers, he started owning the center position when he needed to while still continuing to play like a power forward. He dominated smaller power forwards with his length and strength. Meanwhile, opposing centers could not keep up with his speed and mobility.

So, while Davis plays like an old-school big man in the sense that he can post up and score dominant inside baskets, he still showcases flashes of the modern-day big man by covering the perimeter on defense and making timely jumpers that only a few big men can hit on a consistent basis. In a sense, he represents the evolution of the big man position because he can be a power forward and a center. One could even say that Anthony Davis is the perfect player to label a *forward-center* due to the fact that he knows how to blend the skills of a forward with the dominance of a center to great effect.

With all that said and done, there are no other big men in the history of the NBA that can compare to Anthony Davis's playing style and success in the league. True enough, we've seen our fair share of great big men dominating their way to championships and MVPs. But AD's player profile and talents are simply hard for any other big man to match. And that is precisely why he is one of the NBA's 75 Greatest Players and why he will always be regarded as a trail-blazing big man in the history of the league.

Final Word/About the Author

I was born and raised in Norwalk, Connecticut. Growing up, I could often be found spending many nights watching basketball, soccer, and football matches with my father in the family living room. I love sports and everything that sports can embody. I believe that sports are one of the most genuine forms of competition, heart, and determination. I write my works to learn more about influential athletes in the hopes that from my writing, you the reader can walk away inspired to put in an equal if not greater amount of hard work and perseverance to pursue your goals. If you enjoyed *Anthony Davis: The Incredible Story of One of Basketball's Most Dynamic Power Forwards,* please leave a review! Also, you can read more of my works on *David Ortiz, Cody Bellinger, Alex Bregman, Francisco Lindor, Shohei Ohtani, Ronald Acuna Jr., Javier Baez, Jose Altuve, Christian Yelich, Max Scherzer, Mookie Betts, Pete Alonso, Clayton Kershaw, Mike Trout, Bryce Harper, Jackie Robinson, Justin Verlander, Derek Jeter, Ichiro Suzuki, Ken Griffey Jr., Babe Ruth, Aaron Judge, Novak Djokovic, Roger Federer, Rafael Nadal, Serena Williams, Naomi Osaka, Coco Gauff, Baker Mayfield, George Kittle, Matt Ryan, Matthew Stafford, Eli Manning, Khalil Mack, Davante Adams, Terry Bradshaw, Jimmy Garoppolo, Philip Rivers, Von Miller, Aaron Donald, Joey Bosa, Josh Allen, Mike Evans, Joe Burrow, Carson Wentz Adam Thielen, Stefon Diggs, Lamar Jackson, Dak Prescott, Patrick Mahomes, Odell Beckham Jr., J.J. Watt, Colin Kaepernick, Aaron Rodgers, Tom Brady, Russell Wilson, Peyton Manning, Drew Brees, Calvin Johnson, Brett Favre, Rob Gronkowski, Andrew Luck, Richard Sherman, Bill Belichick, Candace Parker, Skylar Diggins-Smith, A'ja Wilson, Lisa Leslie, Sue Bird, Diana Taurasi, Julius Erving, Clyde Drexler, John Havlicek, Oscar Robertson, Ja Morant, Gary Payton, Khris Middleton, Michael Porter*

Jr., Julius Randle, Jrue Holiday, Domantas Sabonis, Mike Conley Jr., Jerry West, Dikembe Mutombo, Fred VanVleet, Jamal Murray, Zion Williamson, Brandon Ingram, Jaylen Brown, Charles Barkley, Trae Young, Andre Drummond, JJ Redick, DeMarcus Cousins, Wilt Chamberlain, Bradley Beal, Rudy Gobert, Aaron Gordon, Kristaps Porzingis, Nikola Vucevic, Andre Iguodala, Devin Booker, John Stockton, Jeremy Lin, Chris Paul, Pascal Siakam, Jayson Tatum, Gordon Hayward, Nikola Jokic, Bill Russell, Victor Oladipo, Luka Doncic, Ben Simmons, Shaquille O'Neal, Joel Embiid, Donovan Mitchell, Damian Lillard, Giannis Antetokounmpo, Chris Bosh, Kemba Walker, Isaiah Thomas, DeMar DeRozan, Amar'e Stoudemire, Al Horford, Yao Ming, Marc Gasol, Draymond Green, Kawhi Leonard, Dwyane Wade, Ray Allen, Pau Gasol, Dirk Nowitzki, Jimmy Butler, Paul Pierce, Manu Ginobili, Pete Maravich, Larry Bird, Kyle Lowry, Jason Kidd, David Robinson, LaMarcus Aldridge, Derrick Rose, Paul George, Kevin Garnett, Michael Jordan, LeBron James, Kyrie Irving, Klay Thompson, Stephen Curry, Kevin Durant, Russell Westbrook, Chris Paul, Blake Griffin, Kobe Bryant, Joakim Noah, Scottie Pippen, Carmelo Anthony, Kevin Love, Grant Hill, Tracy McGrady, Vince Carter, Patrick Ewing, Karl Malone, Tony Parker, Allen Iverson, Hakeem Olajuwon, Reggie Miller, Michael Carter-Williams, James Harden, John Wall, Tim Duncan, Steve Nash, Gregg Popovich, Pat Riley, John Wooden, Steve Kerr, Brad Stevens, Red Auerbach, Doc Rivers, Erik Spoelstra, Mike D'Antoni, and *Phil Jackson* in the Kindle Store. If you love basketball, check out my website at claytongeoffreys.com to join my exclusive list where I let you know about my latest books and give you lots of goodies.

Like what you read? Please leave a review!

I write because I love sharing the stories of influential athletes like Anthony Davis with fantastic readers like you. My readers inspire me to write more so please do not hesitate to let me know what you thought by leaving a review! If you love books on life, basketball, or productivity, check out my website at claytongeoffreys.com to join my exclusive list where I let you know about my latest books. Aside from being the first to hear about my latest releases, you can also download a free copy of *33 Life Lessons: Success Principles, Career Advice & Habits of Successful People*. See you there!

Clayton

References

[i] *Draft Express*. Web.

[ii] Harper, Zach. "Uniqueness of Anthony Davis' offense is what makes him promising". *CBS Sports*. 17 October 2013. Web.

[iii] Leonardis, Dave. "Why Anthony Davis Will Emerge as a Full-Fledged NBA Superstar in 2013-14". *Bleacher Report*. 7 October 2013. Web.

[iv] Eichenhofer, Jim. "Anthony Davis up to 238 pounds, may still be growing from 6-10". *NBA.com*. 20 June 2014. Web.

[v] Golliver, Ben. "Pelicans hire Alvin Gentry to play faster, fully unleash Anthony Davis". *Golf*. 30 May 2015. Web.

[vi] Eichenhofer, Jim. "Anthony Davis up to 253 pounds while maintaining athletic frame". *NBA.com*. 27 August 2015. Web.

[vii] Greer, Jordan. "Anthony Davis elevates his game, Pelicans' offense with improved passing". *Sporting News*. 9 December 2018. Web.

[viii] Stein, Marc. "Anthony Davis wants out of New Orleans, and the Lakers may be his destination". *New York Times* 28 January 2019. Web.

[ix] "Anthony Davis discusses Los Angeles, LeBron James and more". *NBA.com*. 1 July 2019. Web.

[x] Pina, Michael. "LeBron James has never had a teammate as perfect as Anthony Davis". *SB Nation*. 18 June 2019. Web.

[xi] Medina, Mark. "Anthony Davis says he's '100 percent healthy,' Lakers' title chances higher after hiatus". *USA Today*. 2 July 2020. Web.

[xii] Yip, Sam. "Lakers: Anthony Davis Jumpshot Efficiency is the Worse in the League". *Sports Illustrated*. 27 November 2021. Web.